Many Christians are skeptical about what creativity might do to their faith. At the same time, a lot of creatives worry about what Christianity might do to their talents.

But it doesn't have to be this way.

God and creativity are not in opposition. Far from it. God is the creator of creativity. He made you creative. This is why your creativity needs theology and why your theology needs creativity. If we really want to know and practice creativity to its fullest, we should begin where creativity begins. We should begin with God.

When we do, we find that where many Christians have stayed silent, God still speaks. And where the world so often distorts, God gives clarity.

Now is the time to listen. Now is the time to see creativity from God's perspective.

God is reclaiming creativity for His glory and our good.

Praise for *Images and Idols*

This book is no ivory tower thought experiment. It is tested and proven, lived out in the real world and filled with timeless wisdom.

JASON "PROPAGANDA" PETTY
Rapper, poet, and speaker

What do creativity and art have to do with God? Quite a lot, actually. *Images and Idols* is a book that beautifully shows how faith and art are both stronger when they are in conversation. Theologically rich and yet totally approachable, this is a must-read book for artists and creatives of faith.

BRETT MCCRACKEN
Senior editor, The Gospel Coalition; author of *Uncomfortable; Gray Matters;* and *Hipster Christianity*

What has Hollywood to do with Jerusalem, the studio with the sanctuary? Everything. In *Images and Idols*, Thomas Terry and Ryan Lister take the reader on a journey across the storyline of Scripture, tracing the theme of creativity along the contours of redemptive history. Beginning in Eden, accounting for the fall of humanity, then intersecting the gospel, Terry and Lister demonstrate that creativity not only can be redeemed, but that it must be redeemed if the great Creator is to finish His goal of taking His re-created people to the new heavens and new earth. If you have any creative impulse at all, you should read this book. Christ-honoring and gospel-saturated, with plenty of helpful application, this is biblical theology at its finest.

TODD L. MILES
Professor of Theology, Western Seminary; author of *Superheroes Can't Save You* and *A God of Many Understandings?*

Images and Idols: Creativity for the Christian Life does something that's desperately needed—it connects orthodoxy to art and creativity. Thomas and Ryan construct a solid bridge for the artist and theologian to meet in new ways by showing us that the greatest work for both parties is to know God deeply, the Beautiful One and Creator of all.

Sometimes a book hits you in such a way that you want to purchase it in bulk and give it to all your friends, hoping they too will have the same experience. This was one of those books for me. I praise God for *Images and Idols* and cannot wait to give it to all the artists I know.

ASHTON TRUJILLO
Filmmaker

How should we as evangelicals think about creativity, art, and beauty? Terry and Lister celebrate beauty and creativity, but they also situate them onto the proper theological landscape. Art, beauty, and creativity are for God's sake and for His glory, since all creativity and beauty reflect the creativity and beauty of the Lord. Creativity is not disconnected from the biblical storyline, from creation, fall, redemption, and new creation, as Terry and Lister so eloquently remind us. A foundational book theologically for thinking about beauty, the arts, and creativity.

THOMAS R. SCHREINER
James Buchanan Harrison, Professor of New Testament Interpretation; Associate Dean, The Southern Baptist Theological Seminary; author of *The King in His Beauty* and *Covenant and God's Purpose for the World*

Theology and creativity are intertwined because the subject of theology—God Himself—is the most creative being in existence. One cannot seek to know Him fully without learning something about creativity along the way. Likewise, those who wish to be creative can find no better model than the maker of all things. This book provides pathways in both directions, revealing God as a Creator and all of humanity as creatives. Thomas and Ryan are faithful guides on these intertwining paths, inviting us to love both God and creativity better, and encouraging us to allow that love into better work for God's kingdom and glory.

MIKE COSPER
Founder and director, Harbor Media and Narrativo Group

RECLAIMING CREATIVITY SERIES

IMAGES
AND IDOLS

CREATIVITY FOR THE CHRISTIAN LIFE

THOMAS J. TERRY & J. RYAN LISTER

MOODY PUBLISHERS / CHICAGO

Edited by Kevin P. Emmert
Interior Design: Eleazar Ruiz
Cover Design: Anthony Benedetto
Cover Image: Anthony Benedetto

All websites and phone numbers listed herein are accurate at the time of publication but may change in the future or cease to exist. The listing of website references and resources does not imply publisher endorsement of the site's entire contents. Groups and organizations are listed for informational purposes, and listing does not imply publisher endorsement of their activities.

Library of Congress Cataloging-in-Publication Data

Names: Terry, Thomas J., author. | Lister, J. Ryan (John Ryan), 1978- author.
Title: Images and idols : creativity for the Christian life / Thomas J. Terry and J. Ryan Lister.
Description: Chicago : Moody Publishers, [2018] | Includes bibliographical references.
Identifiers: LCCN 2018031605 (print) | LCCN 2018034331 (ebook) | ISBN 9780802497338 (ebook) | ISBN 9780802418487
Subjects: LCSH: Creative ability--Religious aspects--Christianity. | Creation (Literary, artistic, etc.)--Religious aspects--Christianity. | Christianity and the arts.
Classification: LCC BT709.5 (ebook) | LCC BT709.5 .T47 2018 (print) | DDC 233/.5--dc23
LC record available at https://lccn.loc.gov/2018031605

ISBN: 978-0-8024-1848-7

We hope you enjoy this book from Moody Publishers. Our goal is to provide high-quality, thought-provoking books and products that connect truth to your real needs and challenges. For more information on other books and products written and produced from a biblical perspective, go to www.moodypublishers.com or write to:

Moody Publishers
820 N. LaSalle Boulevard
Chicago, IL 60610

1 3 5 7 9 10 8 6 4 2

Printed in the United States of America

To my wife, Heather Leigh Terry—
Selfless, helpful, gracious, and honest,
wise, winsome, beautiful, and modest.
The one God has most used to grow me in godliness.

———

To my mother, Jane Freeman Lister—
Who knew I'd write this book well before I did,
and who (not-so) quietly prayed it into existence.
I wish I could see the smile on your face.

CONTENTS

FOREWORD

Dear Creative,

I've always found it interesting how the Bible introduces us to God. The first three words are plain, only if not taken seriously. "In the beginning," it says to us. Taking us back to the time when time was not yet. Back when nothing existed except God. God didn't need time to live. Or someone else to bring Him to life. He, in and of Himself, was life. He was here always, and one day, literally, God did something only He could do. He created.

And ain't that something? That by divine inspiration, what is to be known about God, in the first sentence of God's glorious Word is that He is a creator. And a good one at that. One look at the sky will tell you that much. I've sat on the shore of one of His oceans and couldn't help but notice how beautiful water can be when it moves underneath the sun. That wide sea, lit up by that contained fire, too high to singe the earth and low enough to warm the day, are declaring the glory of God (Ps. 19:1) All that He's created is to do the same, including humanity.

Humanity, as we know from Genesis 1:27, was made in His image. As image bearers, we too create. With that being the case, it would be unreasonable to believe that our creativity has nothing to do with God. If anything, it has everything to do with God because it has always belonged to God. Such as when Jesus was asked about whether paying taxes to Caesar was lawful. To which He responded with a question concerning "likeness." He asked them whose likeness was on their money. They answered Him, "Caesar's." Jesus, then, doing as He always does, responded with something sharp and true. He said, "Render to Caesar the things that are Caesar's, and to God the things that are God's" (Mark 12:17). Caesar's likeness may have been on their coins, but God's likeness was on *them* and us. Rendering to God what belongs to Him won't happen as long as humanity in general and creatives specifically assume that they, not God, have claim on themselves and all that they create.

But seeing that God's image is on us, then all that comes out of us is best understood in light of Him and not in spite of Him. It may sound unbelievable, but having a God-centered perspective on creativity benefits all creatives in the long run. Why? Because God created us. And out of us comes various forms of creativity. So understanding God's intent as it relates to our creativity will set us loose to create with clarity and conviction. That's the message of *Images and Idols*. Thomas and Ryan are calling us back to the source of our creativity, God. By doing so, they are helping us to rediscover our creative calling.

In God's kindness, He's given creatives the ability to do what He did in the beginning and what He's being doing since then. Some of us do it by singing songs. Others by painting images or writing poems or books or raps. We, in more ways than one, mirror Him as we do. What a privilege that is! To be welcomed into the work and joy of making something out of nothing and being able, by God's grace, to call it "good" (Gen. 1:31). Clearly, we may not be able to *make* all things new like Him. Or *create* in ourselves a clean heart. Or become a new *creation* at the sound of our own voice. But God is the first Creative and the ultimate source of creativity. Let's look to Him as we try to make heaven and earth with our bare hands.

Sincerely,

JHP

WHY
CREATIVITY
MATTERS
TO US

Reclaiming Creativity began as, and continues to be, a conversation between friends: one who has spent the last two decades in lecture halls and library carrels (Ryan), the other who has spent his life in recording studios and on stage (Thomas). Though our backgrounds differ, our friendship meets at the foot of the cross. We are alike in that we both are sinners clinging to the gospel of Jesus Christ and want to see God's grace reconcile every part of our lives, including our creativity, to Him. Likewise, we believe that God orchestrated our lives to accomplish His great purposes through broken people like us, that He has entrusted us with His Spirit to prepare His church for His kingdom, and that nothing we say or write matters unless it is grounded in God's holy, inspired, inerrant, and authoritative Word. These shared commitments form the centerpiece of our lives, our friendship, and this project. It is also why we worship together on Sundays and work together at Humble Beast.

In this book series, we hope to bring you into our conversation too. Creativity needs a community to flourish—which is why we've written these books together. From the class lectern, creativity can sometimes ring theoretical and distant—like a sculptor telling you what she sees in the stone before her hands ever pick up hammer and chisel. From the stage, we're often *too* close to process, to see, its origins and purposes—it is the sculpture on display without the sculpture explanation. *Reclaiming Creativity* seeks to bring professor and performer into the same space so that God's plans for creativity stand front and center on the stage and in the classroom.

CREATIVITY
BEGINS WITH GOD

W e have a problem—whether we recognize it or not. It has to do with the relationship between Christianity and creativity.

Many Christians have grown suspicious of creatives. And why not? It seems that just about the time we've memorized all the God-centered lyrics on our favorite band's new album, they publicly declare their atheism and turn their art against the church. It happens so often that the satire news site *The Babylon Bee* issued the dishearteningly clever headline, "Christian Recording Artist Still On Track To Renounce Faith By [the End of Year]."[1]

Creativity impedes true spiritual progress, doesn't it? At least that's what a lot of Christians think. Some suppose the Bible teaches us that our creativity and imagination are childish things that we are supposed to put behind us. Sure, they fit in fine in the church nursery, but they don't have a place in the pulpit, right?

This is why countless acts of creativity fill the church's dustbins along the way to (what we think to be) Christian maturity. So many have given up on their creative impulse because someone somewhere has somehow convinced them that creativity is pointless, excessive, immoral, or childish compared to the things of God. At least that is what some Christians think.

The problem goes both ways, however.

A lot of Christian creatives are skeptical of other Christians, too. Many creative believers we've talked to feel undervalued in the church, so much so that the church no longer feels like home for them. It seems the only time the church needs them is when they want someone "artsy" to decorate the sanctuary for the Christmas Spectacular, or when they need a "creative" to be onstage to show the congregation that they can "relate" to the culture and appeal to those "other" generations.

For many creatives, unfortunately, the Christian faith has become more of a stumbling block than a foundation for their lives. This is why many creatives leave the church and her stained-glass windows behind: the same creativity infused in those panes of glass, the ones filling the sanctuary with kaleidoscopic beauty, no longer feels welcome in many modern churches. So, instead of sticking it out, many creatives wander into the secular wilderness to find like-hearted community, often to the demise of their Christian faith.

The suspicions boiling between creatives and Christians is just the symptom of a bigger problem. Both parties have built their assumptions on bad data: that creativity is secular and will never be sacred. Put another way, the problem of the creativity-Christian divide stems from this unfounded and specious commitment: God has nothing to do with creativity, and creativity has nothing to do with God.

———

THE HOPE OF RECLAIMING CREATIVITY

Nothing could be further from God's truth.

While the world distorts creativity and the church at times conceals it, God does the opposite. He speaks to all of life, including the life of beauty and creativity.

This means that if we want to understand our creativity, we must begin with God, the source and culmination of all things creative.

A world without God will always struggle to give you a reason for your creative impulse. Perhaps it's survival or money or power or the self-defeating promise of immortal fame. But a world designed and upheld by God reveals something much more beautiful and profound: *every act of creativity, in its essence, is an act of worship, a doxological expression of your true humanity and purpose.*

Think what would happen if we stepped *toward* God with our creativity rather than sidestep Him. What happens when we see God as the solution to our creativity-faith problem rather than its cause? What happens when we unplug our ears long enough to hear God speak truth over the divide?

When we do—if we finally surrender our selfish ideas of creativity to God—He promises to gives us something better, what He always meant creativity to be.

———

A WAY FORWARD

This is what we mean by *reclaiming creativity*, the concept driving this book series.

This is different from the way the world defines *creativity*. At a secular level, creativity, as Sir Ken Robinson succinctly puts it, is the "process of having original ideas that have value."[2] This human creativity, then, is more a process than an event. You've probably felt this before. Your ideas evolve over time; they change, grow, transform, expand, and develop. Creativity is also a part of what makes us human; it distinguishes humanity from the rest of creation. Each of us is born with a capacity for creativity, which finds expressions in seemingly countless and beautiful ways.

From a secular standpoint, this is a great way to define creativity and what drives creatives. However, we think there is more to it than this. Hence the need to *reclaim* creativity, which, at its core, is a movement back to God's purposes for creativity. This is why we want it "reclaimed." We want what is God's to be God's. But it is also "reclaimed," at a human level, because it seeks to restore our creativity to these original, God-directed objectives.

We are not comfortable ceding creative expressions to the

whims of culture. Reclaiming creativity, therefore, cuts against the grain. In what follows, we hope to get *behind* the earthly confusion over creativity, and back to what really matters: a creativity with God at its center.

We do this because God is the Creator; all creativity stems *from* Him. He is creativity's origin point. No matter how it may seem, God and creativity have never been in opposition; they are, and always have been, connected. Consequently, if we are ever going to understand creativity properly, we need to know God. The reverse is also true. To know God means we have to see Him as the Creator and Lord of everything, including creativity.

Creativity, though, not only comes from God, but also is *for* God. This "why" of creativity is our primary concern. But sin constantly corrupts creativity's purposes. Sinners either make creativity about themselves or they turn creativity into a weapon to use against others. Creativity in our sin-stained hands always becomes self-serving. We rob it of its original intent and deny its place in God's design, and use it instead for our self-serving purposes. Reclaiming creativity, on the other hand, is about reorienting creativity back to God's original and most fulfilling purposes.

Our hope, then, is to help put all acts of imagination and beauty back in their right place—as offerings before God and gifts to the world. Creativity, as God originally envisioned it, follows the trajectory of the greatest commandment. It is *from* God, *for* worship, and *for* service. Vertically, we glorify God through our creativity—we love Him with all of our creative minds, creative hearts, and creative strength. Horizontally, we create beauty in response to God for the love of neighbor and world. In its simplest terms, *creativity, from a God-centered perspective, is any and all works of imagination done for God and for good.* This is the creativity worth reclaiming.

———

A THEOLOGY *for* CREATIVITY

For this reclamation project, we want to address two issues: God's place in our creativity and our creativity's relationship to God. To do this, we've built this book around the framework of the gospel. Each chapter will show how creativity intersects with who our Creator is (God), who we are (Man), what our problem is (Sin), who our solution is (Christ), and where all this leads (New Creation). This approach will show how these biblical truths realign us personally as well as our understanding of creativity.

To be clear, this book is *not* a practical guide. You won't find a manual on how to write songs and novels or redesign your church's foyer as a faithful creative manual here. Others have done this to various degrees of success. We don't want to tell you how to do *your* craft. We want to try to help with the bigger question. Most of us know how to create, but we struggle—or we soon will—with the purpose behind our creative impulse. So rather than showing you *how* to be creative, we want to help you understand *why* you are creative. Ultimately, we hope to help you see that God is for your creativity rather than against it, as long as it flourishes in the freedom of the gospel. Put another way, we want to show you not how to be creative but what creativity has to do with the Christian life and what the Christian life means for your creativity.

What follows, then, is a call to see creativity from God's perspective, the way He intended, and to show how theology and creativity work together for God's glory and the world's good.

So, come and heed His call. Worship God with your creativity. Serve the world with beauty. Create as only a Christian can create. Create because you are a Christian and, because you are a Christian, you can do no other.

There is but one good; that is God.
Everything else is good when it
looks to Him and bad when
it turns from him.

–C. S. LEWIS–

Being near creative people frees
you to think new thoughts. How
much more an encounter with the
living God and his Word?

–TIM KELLER

God did not create man in his own
image. Evidently, it was quite the
other way about . . .

–CHRISTOPHER HITCHENS–

There is no doubt that creativity
is the most important human
resource of all. Without creativity,
there would be no progress, and
we would be forever repeating the
same patterns.

–EDWARD DE BONO–

THE CREATOR
OF CREATIVITY

WHAT GOD
HAS TO DO WITH YOUR CREATIVITY

When it comes to utilizing the power of beginnings, no creative company does this better than Marvel.

By no means are they the first to harness the power of origin stories. From Aristophanes to Virgil, from Homer to Zola, from Dante's *Inferno* to Gaiman's *American Gods*, we've used stories to make sense of the human experience. Origin stories change us because they set out to address our most fundamental questions, questions like: Who are we? Why are we here? Where did we come from? Where are we going?[1] It is why there are ancient stories of the world springing forth from a lotus flower. It is why the Greeks wrote poetry about Prometheus defying the gods by fashioning humanity out of the soil. It is why Goethe personifies the drama of the human predicament in the characters of Faust and

Mephistopheles. And it is why Camus reframes Sisyphus as our modern-day savior, a messiah who counters the world's absurdity simply with his existence.

Origin stories are Marvel's creative genius. In storylines like *Thor* and *The Avengers*, the writers have tapped into our innate human need to know where we come from and modernized it for a contemporary audience. Marvel writers are modern mythmakers who confront our greatest existential problems through visual narrative. Marvel has spent the last few decades rescuing forgotten heroes from forgotten history books by putting them into the panels of the comic book and the digital projectors in the movie theaters right across the street from us.[2]

This is why Marvel has dominated the box office recently. Origin stories are the key that has unlocked an entire generation's loyalty, not to mention our wallets. Over the last fifteen years, Marvel has built an entertainment and film catalog unparalleled in the history of stories, modern film, and now television. Holding it together are the central storylines giving us the backstories of our favorite superheroes and villains. These stories bring our favorite characters to life. They pull the masks off their true identities and uncover their hidden motivations. Because we've been in the seats since the beginning, Marvel executives are banking on the fact that we will stay in our seats as long as they remain true to the characters we first gave our hearts to.[3]

Marvel's modern mythmakers reveal something intrinsic to all of us.[4] We love origin stories because we were made to love them.

We love them[5] because they cast light on our own search for meaning and purpose, which usually involves an extensive excavation of the past. We love them because we are temporal beings. Looking back comes natural to us. We think that knowing our past might bring us closer to the truth in the present. As mythologist Joseph Campbell explains, when we look backwards, "what we are looking for is a way of experiencing the world that will open to us the transcendent that informs it, and at the same time forms ourselves within it."[6] Knowing where we come from helps make sense of the life-giving questions about who we are and where we are going.

This is why some of us have that session with a counselor later today. We need help confronting our personal origin story. If we can just address the past, we feel like the dark clouds of anxiety enveloping our present (and obstructing the horizon) might finally blow over.

We seek our origin stories because we think they can get us out of our not-so-merry-go-round worlds. We believe that they will point us in the right direction, that they form the runner's blocks for our future lives. We investigate our origin stories because we believe, as the philosopher and theologian Søren Kierkegaard said, that "life can only be understood backwards" even while it "must be lived forwards."[7] We can look to the future only when we have taken care of our past.

But here's the irony. While storytellers—like those at Marvel—continue to write, film, sing, and draw origin stories that explain the human experience, we wonder how many have taken the time to explore the *origin story of their own creativity*. Instead, the modern creative community has more often than not replaced the intrinsic search for creativity's starting point with an emphasis on output. We've exchanged a philosophy of creativity for the pragmatism of productivity. The contemporary catchphrase "Never Stop Creating" offers little space to consider where our creativity originates. Our contemporary fascination with creativity's production keeps us so busy that we don't pursue creativity's original purpose. This is creativity's contemporary mission drift: we are concerned primarily with how we are going to fill the shelves rather than why we want to fill them at all. While our portfolios may be full, we will find it tough to explain—beyond subjective or pragmatic platitudes—why our portfolio exists in the first place.

And this lack of an origin story for your creativity shapes you more than you can imagine.

Creativity actually needs direction, which means creativity needs a starting line. Like a traveler on her way, a point of origin helps determine our way. Without a beginning point for our creativity, we end up lost in a wilderness of our own design. We are susceptible to every mirage the culture offers us. Which means we are no longer on our way, or *the* way; it means we are following someone else's way. This haphazard itinerary often has the intersection of exhaustion and superficiality as its final destination.

THE CHARACTER OF CREATIVITY

We want to help you get where you are going, which is why we want to start with your creativity's true origin story, one that clarifies who you are as a creative person and why you even pursue creative work. To do this, we have to pull ourselves away from our own hypnotic self-reflections and look to the source of all creativity, the Trinitarian God revealed in Christian Scripture. The story of your creativity—yes, *your* creativity—begins and ends with God. Every act of creativity (whether we like it or not) proceeds from these familiar words:

In the beginning, God created the heavens and the earth. (Gen. 1:1)

No doubt, barrels of ink have been spilled over the meaning of this renowned sentence. In fact, complete theological systems and world-and-life-views are built on its foundation. Yet often missing in the theological, scientific, and philosophical "shouting match" over this verse is the simple yet profound truth that this sentence confides: *God is creative, and creativity belongs to God.*

The first thing Scripture tells us about God is that He is creative. But our pursuit of a systematized, didactic portrait of God has pushed this attribute into the endnotes of our theological textbooks, if it finds its way in there at all. Though we call Him Creator, seldom do we find creativity credited to Him. But we want to see these come together. We want to show that God's work as Creator flows from His creative nature. We also want to show that God's creativity defines the paradigm of our own creative lives.[8] To know this is to know this simple but misplaced truth:

All creativity begins and ends in God.

God is your creativity's origin story. This is the testimony of creation. Many know creation to be the theater of God's glory. But don't miss the fact that His theater is a product of His creativity as well. In fact, the entire world, from beginning to end, reflects God's creative agency. God builds the stage, fashions the cast, pens the story, and directs His characters to His good and glorious ends. To know creation, then, is to know God, not in full, but in truth. He signs all He makes with His character and purpose. His creative work bears the seal of His eternal power and divine nature (Rom. 1:20). Simply put, everything He makes sings His creativity.

We know this because we see it in our world and read it in His Word. His world demonstrates His creativity while His Word interprets it for us. Both books of God's revelation—creation and Scripture—testify to His creative character and skill.

> *All creativity begins and ends in God.*

Herein lies the lavish nature of God's ways: God not only created creatively but also interprets this creative work in creative ways. Stop for a moment to appreciate what this means. Our Creator puts His creativity on full display in His creation. But then, so we don't miss it, He interprets and explains His creative work for us in Scripture. Simply creating would have been good and sufficient. But like a detailed artist, God wants us to have a kaleidoscopic vision of His creative glory. In His kind providence, the Lord creatively interprets His own imaginative work for us through brilliant images—images *He created* in the first place to help us understand Him and feel the worshipful weight of His creative brilliance.

This truth is on full display in Isaiah 64:8, when the prophet declares, "**But now, O LORD . . . we are the clay, and you are our potter; we are all the work of your hand.**" Here, God uses the poetic metaphor of the relationship between potter and clay to rebuild the hopes of His covenant people. This verse comes on the heels of Isaiah's lament over Judah's stockpile of sin and God's requisite departure from the nation. The prophetic picture of the potter and clay, then, is an encouraging vision. Isaiah uses the imagery to remind his audience (and us today) that God is the one who fashions a people for Himself. God is the potter. He is the creative artist. We are the clay, the work of His hands, a people He creates for Himself whom He will not forsake.

In the passage, God creatively interprets His own creativity. He uses the artistic imagery of potter and clay to demonstrate His creative power and commitment to His covenant people. Remember, too, that God created every aspect of this imagery. God creates Israel, the covenant, the covenant promises, the prophet, the words spoken, and *even the clay, the potter, and the impetus to make pottery are His.* The imagery would remain inaccessible or inapplicable unless God made the reality supporting the employed images. The creative metaphor rings true because God created all aspects of the metaphor to help us understand Him and our relationship with Him. God creates clay and potters for the production of pottery, but He also creates them to embody the permanence of His covenant promises. What emerges then is a cycle of divine creativity that we often miss, confuse, or distort. It goes something like this:

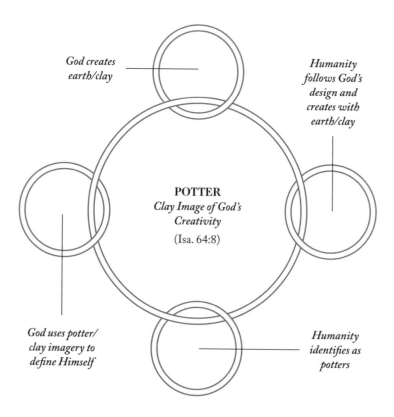

God creates earth/clay

Humanity follows God's design and creates with earth/clay

POTTER
Clay Image of God's Creativity
(Isa. 64:8)

God uses potter/ clay imagery to define Himself

Humanity identifies as potters

God not only demonstrates His creativity in creation but also uses His creation to form the images by which we understand Him as Creator. This is why our creativity sometimes drifts. It lacks its divine anchor point. It doesn't recognize the debt it owes God. Sure, we can be creative outside of Christianity, without recognizing the origin of our creativity, but our work can't help but fall short of its full (and eternal) potential and purpose when we do. God made everything—including His creation and, dare we say, the work of our own hands—to point back to Himself. Creativity makes sense only when it does what it was meant to do.

God the Architect

God, however, doesn't use just one metaphor to display His creativity. He fills the pages of Scripture with images and pictures that make it clear that all creativity begins and ends with Him. If we have eyes to see and ears to hear, God's creative glory is not something we simply recognize; it reframes our own creative lives and helps us understand God Himself.[9]

Take, for instance, the image of God as architect. In his meditation on Psalm 19, John Calvin—a Protestant Reformer *not* known for his gratuitous support of human creativity—reaches for a metaphor to connect his audience with the work of God in creation. What he offers us is a vision of God as the preeminent architect, the one responsible for all the cosmos. For Calvin, though, this was not just a fact; it was a call to worship. "As soon as we acknowledge God to be the supreme Architect, who has erected the beauteous fabric of the universe," writes Calvin, "our minds must necessarily be ravished with wonder at his infinite goodness, wisdom, and power."[10]

What does God's cosmological design do? It shows us God's

glory, helps us grasp His character, and forces us to come to grips with His authority. Calvin is describing what happens when we finally look up at the night sky, miles away from the light pollution of the city. Psalm 19 is about being overwhelmed by reverence for God. It is about God's splendor. Or to sing David's own words: "**The heavens declare the glory of God, and the sky above proclaims his handiwork**" (v. 1). The sky above is a study in architectural expertise that, when witnessed without distraction, makes God's authority palpable and our finitude overwhelming.

God's cosmological design reveals that the world we so desperately (and inadequately) try to control on our own is actually His world and is under His reign. As Calvin helps us see, "the heavens proclaim to us the glory of God, namely, by openly bearing testimony that they have not been put together by chance, but were wonderfully created by the supreme Architect."[11] We didn't make the world, no matter how hard we try to make it ours. The life we live is not even our own, no matter how self-centered we really are. No, it all belongs to its Architect, who builds our world and frames out our lives.

The question is, Do you trust Him to be the Architect of your life? How about of your creative work?

Or do you want only *your* name on the blueprints?

Unfortunately, some of us don't like God being our Chief Architect. We would rather hold that position ourselves. We'd rather keep our heads down and avoid the night sky filled with God's glory, rightfully demanding His praise. We do this by focusing solely on the trivial creative acts of our own doing—the ones dwarfed by God's creative work. We do this to shake our fists at the heavens and declare ourselves the engineers of our own lives—and by relativistic proxy, the rest of the world.

But what happens when we do look up? When we recognize and submit ourselves, and our creativity, to God? We would argue that He includes our designs in His overall blueprints for the world. The two are not opposed. We begin to plan in light of His plans and create in light of His architectural genius. We become junior partners in His architectual firm and help build the kingdom of God through the creativity He has given us.

God's creative design also extends to the world to come. As the author of Hebrews explains, the New Jerusalem, the city-center of the new creation, has God as its **"designer and builder" (Heb. 11:10).** As with the first creation, God is both the new creation's "'architect' (*technitēs*), the planner of each part and integrator of these . . . parts into a whole" and its maker (*dēmiourgos*) who "focuses . . . on the execution of the plans."[12] God goes on to use this architectural imagery to clarify how we become residents of the new heavens and new earth (Heb. 11:16; see also Eph. 2:19–22). Jesus is the once-rejected cornerstone that upholds the new, holy temple of the church, which will populate the new creation (Eph. 2:20–22; see also Matt. 21:42; Mark 12:10; Acts 4:1; 1 Peter 2:6–7). From Scripture's beginning to end, God is the Supreme Architect, who guides and governs His creation into the world that is to come, the world filled with goodness and grace.

God the Artist

God not only plans and builds; He makes everything beautiful. He's concerned not only with making the world, but also with making the world *good*.[13] His creation is attractive, satisfying, and appealing. Why? Because He is the source of all beauty (see Ps. 27:4),[14] and every work of His creative project showcases His character. God's commitment to artistry, in fact, defines the first couple's first home. You see, Eden is more than just a backdrop for the world's beginnings; it's an aesthetics lecture taught in garden form. Every tree, plant, and fruit teaches us that God is the first and true artist, using the garden's form and function to instruct us that God made us to experience His creative beauty. Eden, by God's design, is not utilitarian provision; it is, by God's own description, **"pleasant to the sight"** (Gen. 2:9). This is a garden, not a bleached white cinder-block construction site meant to cloister Adam and Eve away from God and His beauty. There are *no* deficiencies in this garden. Its artist holds nothing back. His perfect beauty is Adam and Eve's only context. His creative splendor is all they know. Like its Creator, Eden is perfect. It is a full-blown garden paradise on the river's edge, teeming with life, lined with monuments of gold and onyx, boasting God's extravagant goodness and glory.

For most, though, the lesson stops here. Many Christians might be thinking, *Okay, okay, we get it. Eden is nice and pretty, but let's get to the snake story in the next part. That's when the action picks up.* We think many of us subconsciously want to fast forward to Genesis 3 because it describes a world closer to our own. But before we turn the page, we need to take a few more steps into Eden.

As with most art, form is driven by function. Eden is no different. The garden's beautiful form follows a more beautiful function. God plants the beautiful garden for a *reason*, and the garden is beautiful for the same reason. Eden provides shelter and nourishment for humanity. But there is more, which we hear in the question, Why did God take the time to make Eden *beautiful*?

To answer this, it helps to see that the two provisions God highlights in the garden are taste and beauty. That which is **"good for food"** is also **"pleasant to the sight" (Gen. 2:9)**. This isn't arbitrary. Instead, Eden shows us that God always intended for life and beauty to be connected. They are a pair. In God's estimation, to know life is to know beauty, and to know beauty is to know life. To know both, then, is to know God's purposes in this world. Eden is the epicenter of life, which means life and beauty are tethered to one another in God.

Eden clarifies that beauty is essential to human experience because beauty is essential to God and His works. Remember who the actor is in Genesis 1–2. God *creates*. God *plants*. God *forms*.[15] God *put* man in the garden. The first couple receives the garden, just as they received every other gift defining their life. God gives it to them. This makes sense of garden life, and it shows us why Eden is more to Adam and Eve than just a first home. The garden's *ultimate* function is to reflect God's beauty. Eden is the world's first art gallery, with God as its artist *and* with God's glory as the medium of His art. God etches His beauty into every living thing. He presses His creativity into every detail of life between the Tigris and Euphrates. He adorns the garden's borders with invasive images of His power, sovereignty, goodness, love, holiness, beauty, and creativity.

Eden's beauty also stems from the fact that the garden's Artist is an artist-in-residence. God plants Adam and Eve in the garden to enjoy His work *and* to enjoy His presence (see Gen. 3:8). The question Eden's beauty whispers is, Why settle just for the divine art when you can *also* have the divine artist? So yes, the garden is the first couple's corner lot with a water view, but the garden's true beauty is God Himself, the one who draws near with both bounty and beauty.

And what is more, the image of God as artist does not die when Paradise is lost. With Adam and Eve forced out of Eden, God continues to work creatively among His image bearers. The work takes on a new purpose; it has a redemptive edge now. Yet His re-creation of man is still an expression of creative skill. As we've already seen, God is the potter fashioning a people for His own possession (Isa. 64:8). He is the one who made us (Ps. 100:3) and He is the one who remakes us. As Paul writes, **"For we are his *workmanship*, created in Christ Jesus for good works, which God prepared beforehand, that we should walk in them"** (Eph. 2:10, emphasis added).[16]

God as Author

While God builds and paints the theater of His glory, He also writes the drama that has played out, is playing out, and will play out across

His stage. God is an author—we know this truth primarily because it is writ large on the pages of divine Scripture. Through the Spirit, God authors the biblical story of our redemption for our knowledge and salvation.

Everything exists because of God's word. As the psalmist exclaims, "**By the word of the LORD the heavens were made, and by the breath of his mouth all their host**" **(Ps. 33:6).** God's word generates. "God's word is creative: he speaks, and it is done; he commands and it stands fast. 'By the word of the Lord were the heavens made, their starry host by the breath of his mouth.' Since God's word is his vocalized breath, it goes forth with the power of his Spirit."[17] The authority of God's word creates all things. This includes humanity, the pinnacle of His creative work. Adam lives because God forms him from the ground and speaks him into existence by breathing life into him.

God's word not only forms the basis for all of creation's existence but also creates the basis for its perseverance. The world endures because God in Christ upholds the universe by the word of His power (Heb. 1:3). The Lord will not put down His pen until His glory fills the pages of history.

He does this primarily by authoring His people's deliverance story. From the outset, God writes His people back to Himself. In Exodus, God writes the holy law to be a "road map" to the enjoyment of God's presence. For Israel, this is more than legal code; it is hope engraved. The written law was the physical identity marker of God's election of the nation, while Israel's law-keeping distinguished them from the pagans and presented the beauty of God's holiness to an onlooking world. The well-documented problem, though, was that Israel, like all of us, went the way of the idols, not the way of holiness.

But that's not the end. God mercifully did not write us out of His story. Instead, He wrote a new covenant. The law His finger engraved on stone (Ex. 31:18) He now etches on the hearts of His new covenant people (see Jer. 31:33; Rom. 2:15).

And how does He do this? Creatively, with His Word. God does more than write our redemptive story; He writes Himself into it. The Word of God writes a way to new covenant redemption. As John tells us, Jesus Christ is God's Word (John 1:1–3), and God's Word was made flesh (John 1:14). Building out of Old Testament images, John boldly humanizes the Word. He shows the *logos* to be a person who simultaneously interprets and reinterprets all that has happened and all that comes after this Jesus Christ, God's Word written into the world.[18] The Word of God enters God's redemptive drama to make a way to the drama's glorious conclusion.

The cross standing at the top of Golgotha is the apex of God's story; the empty tomb is the way to the story's promised end. And in God's impeccable imagination, the Word—the very author of life (Acts 3:15)—also becomes the author and perfecter of our faith (Heb. 12:2). Remember that we are Christ's workmanship, His *poiema* (Eph. 2:10)—the Greek term from which we get our modern English word *poetry*. In a very real way, then, we are Christ's physical poems. We are the living words of the living Word written into the drama of the divine author.

—

CREATIVITY ORIGINATED: GOD THE MASTER ARTIST

Creativity begins and ends with God. This has two implications: one centering on God's glory, the other on His goodness. First, creation perpetually broadcasts God's glory. God paints His *transcendence*— His divine otherness, His holy distinction in nature and worth— into His world with the brush of His creativity. Creation pours forth the divine Author's speech day after day (Ps. 19:2). His glory, in other words, always has been, always is, and always will be evident in His creative work regardless of our response (see Rom. 1–2). His creativity is never not here. He stamps and seals everything He does and everything He creates with His character and beauty.

This leads to the second point. Divine creativity does more than demonstrate God's glory; it demands a response. His creativity must be engaged. God creates and is creative for our enjoyment. This is the *function* of God's creativity: He writes His goodness into His world for our "reading pleasure." As St. Augustine explains, all good things come from God:

> The highest good, than which there is no higher, is God, and consequently He is unchangeable good, hence truly eternal and truly immortal. All other good things are only from Him, not of Him. For what is of Him, is Himself. . . . For He is so omnipotent, that even out of nothing, that is out

of what is absolutely non-existent, He is able to make good things both great and small, both celestial and terrestrial, both spiritual and corporeal [bodily]. . . . [N]o good things whether great or small . . . can exist except from God; . . . all good things, even those of most recent origin, which are far from the highest good, can have their existence only from the highest good [which is God].[19]

Augustine helps us recognize that God *is* goodness and, therefore, the fount of everything good in creation. That means that when we enjoy God's creativity under God's direction, we are basking in God's goodness diffused throughout His creative world. This is why God created us; we've been designed to experience *His* goodness in a variety of ways. It is why we have five senses. We're made to marvel at His glory and goodness with every light wave pouring into our irises and every scent we breathe in. A central purpose in life, then, is to revel in and reflect back to God His creative glory. We were made for this.

If God is the origin point of creativity, then it means that He is the Master Artist. He is the epicenter of all creativity. That means your creativity stems from Him and overflows from His creative work in the world. This has massive implications for who we are as creative beings, what we should do with our creative impulse, and how we use our creativity well. Our creativity makes sense only if it abides in God and points back to Him. This is why most of us avoid the origin story of creativity, because to face it means we have to face our Creator. As sinners, this is often the last thing we want to do. But we can't gloss over how God's creativity reinforces our own. From the resources we use for our imaginative work to the theory informing it, from the philosophy undergirding our creativity to the instinct to create, we cannot escape God. He is the God *of* creativity and the God *behind* our creativity. No matter how hard we try to rewrite our creativity's origin story, it will always begin and end with Him—because all creativity is His.

A Christian should use these arts to
the glory of God, not just as tracts,
mind you, but as things of beauty to
the praise of God.

—FRANCIS SCHAEFFER

The characteristic common to God
and man is apparently that: the desire
to make and the ability
to make things.

—DOROTHY L. SAYERS

—SCOTT DERRICKSON

propaganda.

Art with an agenda is always

IN *DEAD POETS SOCIETY*
—JOHN KEATING

stay alive for.

romance, love—these are what we

to sustain life. But poetry, beauty,

are noble pursuits and necessary

law, business, engineering, these

is filled with passion. And medicine,

the human race. And the human race

poetry because we are members of

because it's cute. We read and write

We don't read and write poetry

2

CREATED
TO CREATE

*WHAT YOUR HUMANITY
HAS TO DO WITH YOUR CREATIVITY*

N o creative company is more perceptive about the human experience than Pixar Studios.

Pixar doesn't just hold up a mirror to their audiences; they shatter it and force us to look beyond our reflection to understand what it means to be human. That's why in most of their films, the characters teaching us about ourselves aren't human at all. Whether it's a toy cowboy (Woody in *Toy Story*), a clownfish (Marlin in *Finding Nemo*), a talking dog (Dug in *Up*) or a rusty, trash-collecting robot (*WALL-E*), Pixar writes our humanity into the most unlikely places and improbable characters to shock us into seeing who we are and where our place in this world really is.

They even go so far as to use a rat to teach us what it means to be human. That's exactly what Pixar is up to in their Academy Award–

winning film *Ratatouille*. This is the simple story of Remy, a rat who wants (and has the chops) to be a gourmet chef like his culinary hero, the French chef Gusteau. *Ratatouille*, though, is more than just another *rodent*-out-of-water tale; it is a cinematic apologetic for human creativity. As Remy explains in the film's opening scene,

> I know I'm supposed to hate humans, but there's something about them. They don't just survive. They discover; they create! I mean, just look at what they do with food![1]

With Pixar's patented irony, a rat forces us to consider how creativity distinguishes our humanity from all other creatures. Remy has aspirations; he doesn't want to live the "rodent way" any longer. He explains to his family that he is "tired of just taking things." He doesn't want to just nose through the trash for his next meal. Rather, Remy wants to create *like humans*. As he explains, "I want to make things. I want to add something to this world."

By design, Remy the rat is more human than most humans. This is exactly the juxtaposition that writer and director Brad Bird was after. For him, *Ratatouille* is "a story about a rat who was trying to move into the human world . . . [a story where] our lead character [chose] to become more and more human."[2] Bird wants this to make us uncomfortable, too. After all, the movie is about a rat in *our* kitchen. "Films . . . thrive on conflict," Bird argues, "and the idea of a rat wanting to be a chef puts two worlds . . . immediately in conflict."[3]

While the tension at the heart of the film's plotline is rodent vs. kitchen/health inspector, a more subtle conflict propels *Ratatouille*'s theme. This is the conflict of creativity: overcoming the insurmountable to create something original. *Ratatouille* uses this conflict to explore the essence of our creativity, a subject very much on the mind of Pixar's brain trust of John Lasseter, Ed Catmull, and former Pixar chairman, Steve Jobs. In fact, if you replaced Paris with Silicon Valley and cuisine with computer-animated storytelling, *Ratatouille* could pass for a documentary on Pixar's own inception. In telling Remy's tale, Pixar subtly records its own history as a fledgling computer animation startup punching at the ankles of movie industry giants to create beautiful and new stories, on their own terms.

This "fight for creativity" instills *Ratatouille*'s pivotal scene with climactic power. Here, the cynical, despotic food critic Anton Ego—the "Grim Eater" of the Parisian culinary scene—stands in direct opposition to Remy's aspirations and, on a deeper level, all creativity's potential. Yet with one nostalgia-filled bite of the rat's ratatouille, Ego's hypercritical walls come tumbling down, leaving him vulnerable to the lure of innovation. With skeletal fingers poised over his typewriter, Ego composes a review that judges— not his rodent adversary, but his own jaded heart, withered by the professional pitfalls of a critic's life. In a speech that only Peter O'Toole's eloquent narration could do justice, Ego explains his metamorphosis, word by beautiful word:

> [T]he bitter truth we critics must face is that, in the grand scheme of things, the average piece of junk is probably

more meaningful than our criticism designating it so. But there are times when a critic truly risks something, and that is in the discovery and defense of the new. . . . Last night, I experienced something new, an extraordinary meal from a singularly unexpected source. To say that both the meal and its maker have challenged my preconceptions about fine cooking is a gross understatement. They have rocked me to my core. . . . Not everyone can become a great artist, but a great artist can come from anywhere. It is difficult to imagine more humble origins than those of the genius now cooking at Gusteau's, who is, in this critic's opinion, nothing less than the finest chef in France. I will be returning to Gusteau's soon, hungry for more.

No wonder this quote is one of Pixar cofounder Edwin Catmull's "favorite moments in any Pixar movie."[4] Ego just narrated Catmull's own arduous creative journey. In many ways, Catmull *is* Remy—one with limitless gifts consistently overlooked because he didn't fit Hollywood's preconceived notions. And while Catmull is Remy, we might say Steve Jobs is his Anton Ego, the critical insider willing to buck the (or create a new) system to back Pixar's "me-against-the-world" dream. Catmull even uses Ego's own words to describe the creative vision for Pixar when he explains, "Originality is fragile. . . . [T]he *new needs protection*. . . . And protection of the new—of the future, not the past—must be a conscious effort."[5]

In the end, though, Ego's speech is not ultimately about cooking;

it's about the creativity that makes all of us *human*. *Ratatouille* gives us much more than a warm-hearted story about a rat who loves to cook. It's more than a creative retelling of a computer animation studio's David-versus-Goliath fight against Hollywood's machine to get their stories heard. Fundamentally, Pixar is telling us our own story, a strikingly designed lesson on what it means to be human and what creativity means for our humanity.

_____

CREATED *FOR* CREATIVITY: DOING WHAT WE WERE MADE TO DO

Like all good creatives,[6] Pixar works off of borrowed material. They don't preach digital sermons about their own brand of a new and improved anthropology.[7] If they did, Pixar couldn't keep the sugar-fueled kids in their theater seats (or their parents off their smartphones) like they've been able to do. Instead, their films resonate and endure because they exegete what we all have in common. Their films use charm and magic to remind us of our humanity. Frame by frame, film by film, Pixar *reenchants* us with what makes us human— our very essence that we sometimes impulsively exchange for to-do lists, paychecks, and the opinions of others.

The Image of God

In other words, Pixar movies work because they show us what we were made for and what we were made to do. As charismatic as

Remy and WALL-E are, though, they—like the rest of the Pixar team—can teach us only part of our anthropology. We need the rest of the lesson to move us from creativity's *what* to creativity's *why*. To know ourselves in full, we need to understand not only the *manner* of our creativity, but also the *reason* for it.

We believe creativity actually flourishes when it has a purpose, especially one that is bigger than those of our own making. We believe there is a true fountainhead for our imaginative lives that offers a better reason than doing it for money or fame. If we can shrug off our secular and postmodern lethargy, wisdom will inevitably lead us back to page 1 of our Bibles and, by design, back to God.

As we saw in the last chapter, God is the origin of creativity. Everything exists because of God. He speaks it into being; everything matters because He fills everything with purpose. This is critical if we are going to understand our humanity and, by extension, our own creativity. "If as the Bible teaches, the most important thing about man is that he is inescapably related to God," reasons theologian Anthony Hoekema, "we must judge as deficient any anthropology which denies that relatedness."[8] This means that we, along with our creativity, require divine interpretation. As John Calvin recognized at the beginning of his *Institutes*, "Man never achieves a clear knowledge of himself unless he has first looked upon God's face, and then descends from contemplating him to scrutinize himself."[9] We cannot know ourselves, therefore, without knowing God.

God holds the key to your self-understanding because He created you *in His own image*. To know yourself then means we need to return to Genesis 1, the beginning of our understanding of both God *and humanity*. In the middle of the creation account, Genesis 1 breaks its narrative to announce poetically,

> **So God created man in his own image,**
> **in the image of God he created him;**
> **male and female he created them. (v. 27)**

This is lyrical theology at its finest. In this brief stanza, God details the pinnacle of His creative work. He creates the characters who will act out His drama in the theater of His creation. God casts these characters as male and female representatives of Himself. The Lord of the universe makes us to mirror His glory in His universe. We are also to reflect the world's praises back to Him (see Isa. 43:21). Being the image of God—or the *imago Dei*—means we are localized, finite reflections of His unlimited and infinite transcendence in His creation. We cannot escape the reality of God, because every face in every crowd confronts us with His likeness.

Imaging God, as Genesis 1:27 reveals, is the essence of our humanity. Our struggle, though, is figuring out exactly how we do this. As usual, the surrounding verses prove to be a reliable (and inspired) guide. Back in verse 26, God describes His creation of humanity, declaring, **"Let us make man in our image, after our likeness. And let them have dominion [over all created things]."** Later, in verse 28, God speaks to our humanity once again, this time to bless us and command us to **"be fruitful and multiply and fill the** earth and subdue it, and have dominion [over all created things]."

Amidst the theological complexity in these verses, one thing is clear: God marries our image to our vocation. In three short verses, bearing God's image *(şě·lĕm)* comes up three times (four if you include "likeness" as a synonym) while the work of dominion bookends the *imago Dei* "poem" in verse 27. This repetition and structure are intentional. They reveal that, at a fundamental level, bearing God's image means exercising rule over God's creation. It means acting like God in God's world on God's behalf under God's authority.

This is what theologians have termed the *functional* model of the image of God. And though this theory doesn't capture every nuance of being made after God's likeness, it emphasizes the biblical connection between the *imago Dei* and God's mission in and through us (see Gen. 1:26–28; 2:15; 5:1–3; 9:6; Ps. 8:5–6). What God makes us to do in His world is a critical part of what God makes us to reflect to the world. The image of God, therefore, is very much about exercising godlike rule over God's creation as His ordained representatives.

> *We cannot escape the reality of God, because every face in every crowd confronts us with His likeness.*

The Image of God and Creativity

You might be thinking, *This is all well and good, but what does any of this have to do with my creativity?* This is where *reclaimed creativity* enters the picture. To understand our own creativity, we need to see that it is sourced in God and recognize how our Creator's creativity affects our own.

Reclaimed Creativity Is Biblical. First, the notion of the *imago Dei* isn't something cooked up by a detached, ivory-tower theologian needing an obscure topic for a book that will assure tenure. The image of God was God's idea, meaning that if we are going to understand ourselves, and our creativity, we need to hear what God has to say about us. The image of God tells us that the uniqueness of our humanity—the very thing that differentiates us from the rest of creation—is that we mirror God to His world. We represent Him in our lives and actions. We represent Him with our creativity.

Reclaimed Creativity Is a Divine Instrument. Second, the image of God *unites* God's creativity to our own. Think about what's happening in Genesis 1 leading up to all this *imago Dei* talk. To know how we are like God, we have to ask, What is the central thing we know about God up to this point in Scripture?

Very simply, it is that God creates. It is in God's nature to make things.

Dorothy Sayers, a close friend to C. S. Lewis and J. R. R. Tolkien, and a brilliant author in her own right, makes this connection:

> Looking at man, [the author of Genesis] sees in him something essentially divine, but when we turn back to see what he says about the original upon which the "image" of God was modeled, we find only the single assertion, "God

created." The characteristic common to God and man is apparently that: the desire and ability to make things.[10]

God's creativity defines and informs our creativity. Not only that, He makes us instruments to continue His own creative purposes in His creation. God makes us to make things, just as He makes things. He even commands us to do so. When God tells us to be fruitful and multiply, He's telling us to create more image bearers who will fill the world with God-oriented, God-authorized creativity. When He commands us to exercise dominion, He enlists us as creative agents to care for His creation in imaginative ways.[11]

Reclaimed Creativity Is Derivative. Third, the image of God shows us that our creativity is derivative. Only God's creation is *ex nihilo* (out of nothing), which means our creativity is never purely our own; it relies on our Creator and builds out of His creation. As His image bearers—created by God to be like Him—our creativity *reflects* His. It's not superfluous. Nor does it belong exclusively to us. Rather, our creativity is part of our image bearing. It should, therefore, extend from His authority, and culminate in His objectives.

When it comes to being created in God's likeness, most Christians tend to overemphasize the divine-human parallels to the point that many, if not all, distinctions are lost. The image of God, though, is as much about divine-human contrast as it is about divine-human similarity. God makes us in His "likeness;" we bear His "image." We are like God, but we are *not* God. We bear His image, but not His essence. We are dynamic copies that God designed to *represent*—not *replace*—the original in His creation.

Think about the raw materials for your creativity. These originate in and belong to the Lord of heaven and earth. God bends the knee of our creativity to Himself when He declares,

> Heaven is my throne,
>> and the earth is my footstool;
> what is the house that you would build for me,
>> and what is the place of my rest?
> *All these things my hand has made,*
>> and so all these things came to be.
>> (Isa. 66:1–2, emphasis added)

In His wisdom and grace, the Lord directly or indirectly gives us everything we use to make things. So, if you want to change the color of an image, you don't "invent" the idea of color; you work within the color spectrum you've received and apply it resourcefully. Or if you're creating a monster for a short story, you mix up established parts into a new creature (for example, green, horned, sharp teeth, and wings). J. R. R. Tolkien calls our imaginative appropriation of God's handiwork "sub-creation." We submit our "fantasy worlds" to the Creator's original because as image bearers we are the copy, and so is our creative output. Tolkien explains, "We make . . . because we are made: and not only made, but made in the image and likeness of a Maker."[12] Our creativity, therefore, relies on and submits to the One whose image we reveal. Consequently, our creative work will always have a double signature: ours as an apprentice and God's as divine Master.

Reclaimed Creativity Is Freedom. Fourth, the image of God makes a way for true creative freedom. At first, this may seem contradictory, but, in Christianity, the submission of our creativity actually prepares the way for your creative freedom. As Francis Schaeffer puts it,

> Trumpets, cymbals, psalteries, harps, all the various instruments of David—music upon music, art upon art— all pouring forth, all pointing up the possibility of creativity in praise of God, all carried to a high order of art at God's command. And when you begin to understand this sort of thing, suddenly you can begin to breathe, and all the terrible pressure that has been put on us by making art something less than spiritual suddenly begins to disappear. And with this truth comes beauty and with this beauty a freedom before God.[13]

All of this beauty stems from God's creative rights *over* you. The image of God reveals this in two ways. The first is the cause and basis for our image bearing: God's elevated status over those whom He makes in His image. The second way results from the first: man's image bearing of God elevates his status over the rest of creation. This reveals an ordered world and a natural submission—one that exists before sin, not because of the fall. This order establishes God's creative rights over all He's made, especially those whom He made in His likeness.

We all recognize this: if you make something, it belongs to you. This is why, in 2015, a jury awarded nearly $7.4 million to the estate of Marvin Gaye. The court determined Robin Thicke and Pharrell Williams plagiarized Gaye's 1977 song "Got to Give It Up" without permission for their massive 2013 summer hit, "Blurred Lines."[14] With creation comes ownership. God is our maker; we are not His maker. Our lives—our very image—rely solely upon His creative and providential rule. Therefore, He has rights over us and our creativity. From the beginning, God designed us to live happily under His dominion as we happily reflect God by creatively exercising dominion over His creation.

For this reason, our imaginative lives are most in order when they're seen through the lens of the Creator-creature distinction. We must submit our creativity to God. When we do, our imagination does what it was made to do. When we don't, our creativity, at best, becomes ineffective; and, at worst, it usurps God and wreaks havoc on our whole lives. As Solomon articulates,

> Unless the LORD builds the house,
>> those who build it labor in vain.
> Unless the LORD watches over the city,
>> the watchman stays awake in vain. (Ps. 127:1)[15]

This is not a contradiction, but a paradox. When we submit our creativity to our Creator, we finally gain real creative freedom. Our creativity can accomplish its ultimate purpose only when it works within God's design. If we want to truly make things, we need to apprentice under the Master. We were made to create, but our creation was always meant to be from the Lord, to the Lord, and through the Lord.

When we create in the image of our Creator, our creativity is no longer enslaved to our self-centeredness, dead-end objectives, or limited influence. Instead, it is free to be what God intended our creativity to be: God-centered, divinely directed, and eternally influential.

Sometimes we need to see our creativity from another angle. Think of it this way:

O n the back shelf, in a dark corner of your favorite antique shop, you find a folded canvas buried under a layer of dust. At first glance, it seems quite unspectacular. But when you look past the tattered and frayed edges, it steals your attention. You want to know what it would look like in the light. You want to see what the rest of the canvas has to offer. Intrigue leads you to the sales counter, and when you finally get home, you eagerly begin to unfold your canvas. This seems to take forever. The sheer size of the canvas forces you to finish the job outside. When you're finally done, the sheet covers your front lawn completely. But it doesn't matter, because laying before you is the most magnificent design you've ever seen. The sight of it entrances you. Soon, a crowd gathers and they, too, tell you how beautiful it is. But as the day passes by and the sun begins to go down, the crowd dwindles until it's just you and your canvas alone again.

Or so you thought. Right as you begin to fold up your prized possession, an old man steps toward you. You remember him from the crowd because he was the only one who never looked at the canvas. He stared at you the whole time. His coarse voice disrupts the silence.

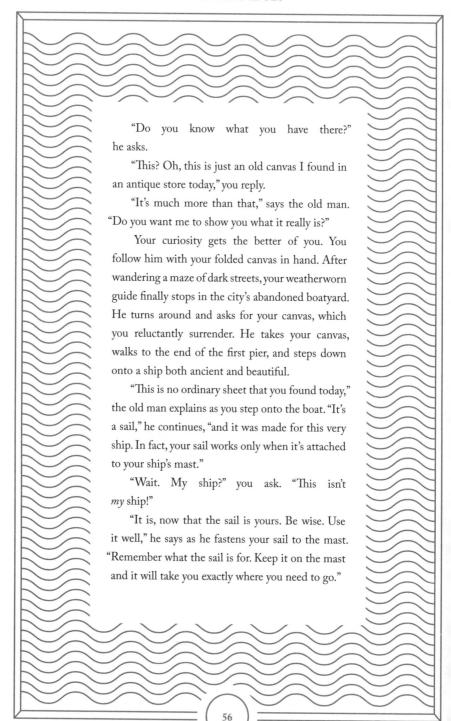

"Do you know what you have there?" he asks.

"This? Oh, this is just an old canvas I found in an antique store today," you reply.

"It's much more than that," says the old man. "Do you want me to show you what it really is?"

Your curiosity gets the better of you. You follow him with your folded canvas in hand. After wandering a maze of dark streets, your weatherworn guide finally stops in the city's abandoned boatyard. He turns around and asks for your canvas, which you reluctantly surrender. He takes your canvas, walks to the end of the first pier, and steps down onto a ship both ancient and beautiful.

"This is no ordinary sheet that you found today," the old man explains as you step onto the boat. "It's a sail," he continues, "and it was made for this very ship. In fact, your sail works only when it's attached to your ship's mast."

"Wait. My ship?" you ask. "This isn't *my* ship!"

"It is, now that the sail is yours. Be wise. Use it well," he says as he fastens your sail to the mast. "Remember what the sail is for. Keep it on the mast and it will take you exactly where you need to go."

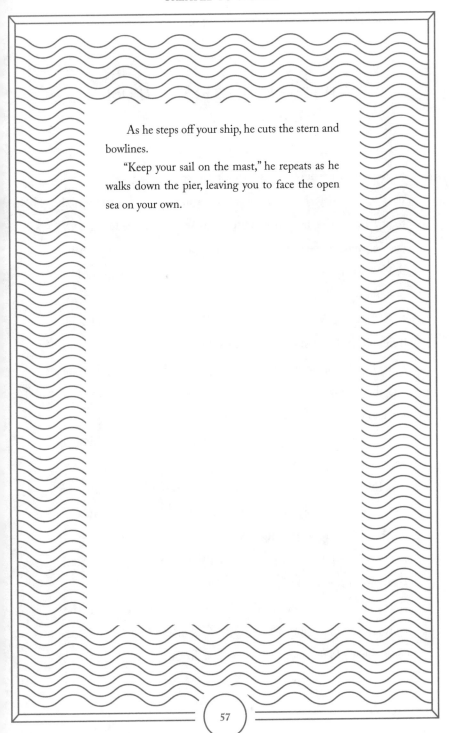

As he steps off your ship, he cuts the stern and bowlines.

"Keep your sail on the mast," he repeats as he walks down the pier, leaving you to face the open sea on your own.

CREATIVITY REFLECTED: PURPOSE OF HUMAN CREATIVITY

Like your canvas sheet, your creativity needs appropriate structures to recognize its design and accomplish its purpose. God doesn't restrict creativity; He frees and ensures it. Only when submitted to the Lord does our creativity take us where we need to go. Of course, we can use it for other means, but it will never reach its full, maximum, eternal potential until it's coupled to God and His mission.

Please don't misunderstand us. Each of our sails will look different, and our ships will chart different courses from time to time. But the same structure and purpose is always there. The sail and the ship work in tandem. God made our creativity to work in tandem with Him. Put another way, as a sail needs a ship to get you to your destination, your creativity needs God to fulfill its design and unique purpose in His world.

This is why St. Augustine's famous prayer applies to all of us *and to our creativity*: "because you have made us for yourself, and our heart is restless until it rests in you."[16] As God makes each of us for Himself, He makes our creativity for the same reason. Your creativity, therefore, works only when it rests in God and you tether your purposes to His own. This is true freedom,[17] and this is the truly creative life: using our God-given creativity to glorify Him and serve the world through beauty and imagination.[18]

The Greatest Commandment of Creativity

Our creativity exists to spread beauty through the prism of the greatest commandment. Christ's words realign everything, including our creative lives:

> "You shall love the Lord your God with all your heart and with all your soul and with all your mind. This is the great and first commandment. And a second is like it: You shall love your neighbor as yourself. On these two commandments depend all the Law and the Prophets." (Matt. 22:37–40)

Here, Christ turns the world right-side up again. He unites two Old Testament laws and puts love in the middle. He sets our hearts, souls, and minds on loving God and neighbor. This is the essence of life in God's kingdom and the purpose of our humanity and, therefore, our creativity. The greatest commandment reveals that every part of humanity—including (and especially) our creativity—exists to bring God glory and ensure our neighbor's good. God, then, makes us to worship Him and serve other image bearers. And to do just this, God gives us creativity.

Creativity for God's Glory

The image of God, therefore, has everything to do with God's glory. In a God-ordained and finite way, we make the Invisible, visible. We are living icons[19] of the God Most High, set on earth to represent

His glory and exemplify His reign. As Tolkien captures in *The Lord of the Rings*, we are all Denethors—stewards of Gondor—sitting under the rightful Sovereign's throne, ruling on His behalf, under His authority, ever looking to the horizon for the return of our King.[20]

Our creativity is like a spark floating on the winter wind. On its own, it offers merely a flicker of light and heat, but its power lies in its promise of the fire that produced it. We want our creativity to reflect the wildfire of God's glory.

> *Creativity helps open heaven's doors to let the light of God's transcendence flood into our head-down, cynic-filled world. We make things to help the world look up.*

In fact, creativity is the way we know anything about God's glory. Tim Keller contends, "It takes the imagination to sense something has meaning because we cannot cognitively grasp the glory of God. The glory of God is beyond our ability to understand or describe. The imagination goes beyond what we can think of and rises to lofty heights where it contemplates the glory of God."[21] Creatives, therefore, create in order "to stimulate that imagination and to show us that things have meaning."[22]

From this perspective, creativity enchants the world with God's glory. Imagination becomes the human work of bringing the eternal into our heads and putting our heads into the eternal. If our creativity rests in His, then our creativity can begin to help make the mundane transcendent, and help bring the transcendent near. As

Anne LaMott summarizes, "Awe is why we are here,"[23] and, in the right hands, our creativity can be a divine instrument that distills hope. Creativity helps open heaven's doors to let the light of God's transcendence flood into our head-down, cynic-filled world. We make things to help the world look up.

Imagination moves us beyond our limitations. It can take us anywhere we want to go, places where we can fly, walk in space, travel through time, and "create" new worlds. Our creativity "works" when it lines up with David's poetic goal to make **"the whole earth . . . filled with awe at your wonders; where morning dawns, where evening fades, you call forth songs of joy"** (Ps. 65:8 NIV). We want others to find these "somethings" bigger than, better than, and beyond this world. This is why creatives have a "special capacity to recognize the 'other country' and communicate with the rest of us regarding the greater reality."[24] You create for the world you were made for and the world that is coming again. Remember where your gospel ends: it's where heaven and earth meet and where God dwells in the midst of His people eternally. Creativity is a mechanism for "seeing" this coming kingdom and the way it breaks into the here and now. It is a bridge between these two worlds, ushering the transcendent into our ordinary, everyday lives while turning our ordinary everyday lives into something transcendent.

This doesn't mean you have to hide a Bible verse in every one of your creative works. God Himself creates beauty for its own sake—because it's ultimately *all* for His sake. As we saw in the last chapter, His creativity flows from His nature; it's why the heavens declare

His glory and the sky proclaims His handiwork (Ps. 19:1). As image bearers, then, our creativity should follow His lead. Some acts, like His work in creation, will whisper His glory; others, like Scripture, will shout it.

Another way to put it is to say that some projects will be like a tree. We love a tree's shade, its limbs that our kids climb, and its autumn-painted leaves. Yet how many of us ever give its root system a second thought? But regardless of our consideration, the tree's roots actually make all the things we love about the tree possible. At times, our creativity will be like this. We will make things marked by beauty, ingenuity, and promise, which will not directly evidence God's purposes but are only available because of Him.

Other projects are like the documentary on the forest that builds its narrative around the indispensability of the trees' root system for the ecosystem's survival. The first hour consists of subterranean footage highlighting the complexities of each tree's particular root patterns as a metaphor for life's rich diversity. Our creativity will follow a similar arc from time to time. As believers, we need to use a portrait lens to see and display God's glory in our work. We will not only evidence God in our creativity, but we seek to spotlight it and give it center stage.

These two are not at odds, nor do they need to be seen as an either/or option. God made us for both. At its most basic level, then, our image bearing demands that every creative act be worthy of our King in its own way and its own design. Not only that, we must recognize that every work of our hands is only possible because we

are the work of His. This is no restriction; this is a privilege. We create *as* the image of God, not in opposition to it. We create *because* of the image of God, not without it. We are free, therefore, to explore God's glorious world and ways from a variety of perspectives, as long as we secure our creativity to God's glory. When done rightly, every song is a worship song, every poem a love poem. They may take different forms and directions but, for the Christian, they all ultimately end up in the same place and are written for the same reason—God's glory.

Creativity for the World's Good

And the good of our neighbor.

One painful experience in a father's life is stepping on his children's Legos. In my (Ryan's) house, I've found the best way to stop this is with an eye roll–inducing lecture for the culprits. I call it the construction-versus-deconstruction talk. My kids have heard it so many times they can recite it verbatim now. In it, I preach the rightness of building good things with their Legos and tell them that though deconstruction is necessary at times, it should always lead to a new project or, at the very least, a clean construction site for the next build.[25]

The fact that they've memorized my lecture shows you just how effective it is. But even though it doesn't ensure pain-free walking in our home (our house shoes do this), it still makes sense to them, even to the youngest. I think this is because being makers, builders, and creators is something innate in all of us. Like Remy in

Ratatouille, we all want to contribute something to the world. We want to give others joy with our work. In fact, at a very fundamental level, we create because it makes us happy to make the world happy. That is why the first thing kids say when they're finished building something with Legos is, "Hey, Mom and Dad, come see what I've made!" They don't realize it, but they're doing exactly what God made them to do: create things to better the world. It starts in their rooms with a small audience but extends outward as they grow and mature in age and ability.

This Lego experience is a microcosm of the *imago Dei's* place in human flourishing. Remember your mandate. You exist to expand God's rule over all the earth. True, we do this to demonstrate God's glory, but also because we are convinced that God is the ultimate source for our and our neighbor's good. God's command to expand His kingdom brings happiness and wholeness to those bending the knee to the King.

So, as we exercise dominion, we actually love our neighbor. We do not bear the image of God to serve ourselves. Being made in God's image is a divine gift, an honor bestowed upon us to play a principal part in filling creation with God's glory and making paradise a part of the human experience. Your imagination is an instrument for this. God uses it to fulfill His mission, which, in His brilliant providence, often includes our happiness. Here is how this works:

1. God creates us with creativity to reveal His glory as stewards of His rule.

2.   We use our creativity to extend His rule in His world.

3.   Our creative acts done to extend God's rule usher joy into the world for our neighbor.

4.   Our creativity expresses our love for neighbor and brings glory to God as our neighbor enters the kingdom.

5.   God's glory is revealed and extended, and, at the same time, our joy is made complete.

So, to borrow again from the great anthropologist Remy, there *is* something about humans. We don't just survive, we create. As we create beautiful things, we serve our neighbors. They are confronted with God's transcendence. They see God's reflection in our image bearing. As we extend God's rule, we extend human flourishing, because where God's kingdom expands, so too does human happiness. With our creativity, we seek to preserve God's image on His earth,[26] to care for our neighbor and to connect our human worth with the worthiness of God. We demonstrate the dignity of our neighbor's life through our creative work and we work creatively to protect our neighbor's dignity. Through all of this, we seek to cultivate a culture centered on loving the God we image and those living in the culture.[27] Simply put, we seek to spread God's kingdom. By reclaiming creativity, the glory of God enchants creation while the love of God and love of neighbor enchants His image bearers' hearts.

Idolatry is worshipping anything
that ought to be used, or using
anything that is meant to be
worshipped.

–ST. AUGUSTINE

These things—the beauty, the
memory of our own past—are
good images of what we really
desire; but if they are mistaken
for the thing itself, they turn into
dumb idols, breaking the hearts of
their worshipers.

–C. S. LEWIS–

PARADISE LOST
–LUCIFER IN
serve in Heaven.
Better to reign in Hell, than to

–JOHN KEATS
Beauty is truth, truth beauty.

3

THE CORRUPTION
OF CREATIVITY

*WHAT SIN
HAS TO DO WITH YOUR CREATIVITY*

N o company captures the current ethos of creativity better than Metro-Goldwyn-Mayer.

They even made it into a logo.

If you've been to the movies anytime since 1924, you've likely seen an MGM film,[1] and you're probably familiar with their iconic roaring lion trademark. But there is more to MGM's opening credits than the lion. Their icon also contains an overlooked but influential statement on creativity. While the lion's roar may steal our attention, the Latin phrase *Ars Gratia Artis* inscribed on the logo's banner captures art's contemporary essence. "Art for Art's Sake," as it's translated, prefaces every MGM film. It stamps each MGM project with their mission statement on creativity. The Latin—not the lion—roars loudest. The phrase announces MGM's resolve to make art completely free from all political, social, religious, and financial agendas. The justification for film, according to Metro-Goldwyn-Mayer's logo, is art and art alone.

At least in principle.

That's because Metro-Goldwyn-Mayer didn't create this philosophy.[2] They were just smart enough to recognize the culture shift and, with a twist of irony, turn it into a marketing catchphrase. "Art for Art's Sake" is bigger than an advertising axiom; it's a defining movement for a generation of artists. Its core conviction is that creativity serves no master but itself. Creativity stands on its own and serves as its own objective. It is independent and self-sovereign.

At least in principle.

That's because the plea for agenda-less art became a revolutionary agenda of its own. "Art for Art's Sake" is a core strand of modern art's DNA. It shapes the way creatives understand themselves and their task. It has redefined art altogether. Art, once centered on results-oriented craftsmanship, is replaced by High Art interested only in making art with no strings attached. The creative who once sought to make "things according to certain rules" in order to "build a chest, to make a wrought-iron gate, to cast a bronze candlestick . . . to make a saddle in leather"[3] is no longer considered an artist. "Art for Art's Sake" forced art to exchange its practical emphasis for its own autonomy and self-determination.

This commitment didn't just change art; it arguably broke it. One of the most public fractures took place in 1917, when the Society of Independent Artists' call for new artwork was met with a piece entitled

Fountain—that now-infamous upside-down urinal that French artist Marcel Duchamp pseudonymously signed "R. Mutt, 1917." From the beginning, the Society's board had promised to display all art submissions as long as the application fee was paid. Duchamp's urinal forced the board's hand; but, more importantly, it forced the art world to answer the question, What is art? When the Society finally rejected *Fountain*, one sector of artists braved an answer. They argued that it was a urinal and not art. But Duchamp, a member of the board, revealed that it was his piece and resigned his post immediately in protest, taking the majority of artistic opinion with him.

Like the urinal on display, *Fountain* turned the creative community upside down. By "transforming" something as functional as a bathroom fixture into art with a simple turn and signature, Duchamp deconstructed everything High Art held dear. *Fountain*'s willed absurdity forced the "Art for Art's Sake" crowd to accept the very thing they rejected in order to define their movement as High Art again. The mundane was now able to be High Art simply because an artist of Duchamp's caliber "chose" it out of a plumbing supply store and signed it with a false name.

As a result, "Art for Art's Sake" mutated into "Art Because the Artist Says So." You could imagine what this did for the artist. Their studios and workshops became the culture's thrones and temples. Art's pragmatic and aesthetic pursuit gave way to its very own quasi-religious perception, with the creative on

> *Self-determination is always the seedbed of idolatry.*

the altar. Almost overnight, creatives became the world's "genius . . . with very special gifts [who] could give mankind something of almost religious importance in . . . the work of art."⁴ That is why creatives and artists today don't simply reflect or serve the culture; they determine it. They fill the world's spotlight and hold the world's microphone. They stand before the world—as clichéd as it has become—as the culture's prophets and, perhaps even to a greater extent, as the gods we can catch a glimpse of in the mirror. "Art for Art's Sake" turned creativity into its own cult and the creative into the culture's high priest and demigod. In making new idols for the world, creatives have been made new idols by the world.

THE BEGINNING OF IDOLATRY

Self-determination is always the seedbed of idolatry.

This isn't just written in MGM's opening credits or the impulse of modern art; it's been this way since the snake snuck into the garden. It's the lie he whispered into Eve's ear with those fateful words, **"You will be like God" (Gen. 3:5)**. It's the greatest bait-and-switch of all bait-and-switches. The serpent promised Adam and Eve autonomy and freedom but delivered guilt and enslavement instead. Forgetting that God had already made them after His likeness, they exchanged their Creator for a forked-tongued lie.

The first couple's rebellion against God turned out to be a rebellion against themselves. Their effort to take God's place at the center of the universe sent their world and lives careening out of orbit. That is even more reason to be in awe of God's response to Adam's and Eve's defiance.

Both punitive and gracious, God doesn't give up on humanity. He punishes sin while still writing us into His story. For all of us found in Adam, the penalty for rebellion hits us in our image. Yes, pain mars our ability to be fruitful and multiply, and the sweat of our brow is the fuel for exercising dominion, but God never erases hope. So while God's punishment is swift and just, He frames it with His mercy. God's mission in the world graciously continues, and so do we. Even death, the death we rightfully deserve, is not the *final* answer. Instead, God promises to take one from Eve's line to do what Adam and Eve could not do: to image God perfectly, crush the serpent, and spread God's kingdom into all the cosmos (Gen. 3:15).

Still, what was done was done. Adam had turned the world upside down. He tossed aside God's perfect kingdom for a counterfeit, broken-down empire that would make him like God (Gen 3:5).

Or so he thought.

Neither Adam nor Eve—nor you nor I—were ever meant to be the center of God's world. We don't have the gravitational pull strong enough to keep everything in its right place. We can't even find our keys in the morning. Ever since our ancestors reached for the forbidden fruit, though, we all have tried to usurp God in some form or fashion. That first temptation spread like a disease to all Adam and Eve's descendants, including you and me. And, like our first parents, we've made a wreck of things. This happens when the finite tries to supplant the infinite. Though none of us would ever try to replace the sun with the moon, we are all hell-bent on replacing God as the center of our lives. Because of sin, we want to worship something less, which, most often, turns out to be ourselves.

The problem, of course, isn't the desire to worship; God made us to be worshipers. Instead, the problem is that we worship the wrong things. Drunk on our false sense of autonomy, we've deluded ourselves into thinking that we are sovereign enough to determine what deserves our worship. If we weren't squinting through sin-cursed eyes, we could see how shortsighted this is. Anything truly worthy of worship will never have its worth conferred to it by its worshipers. Real worship is never democratic. We don't vote on what or who merits our devotion. No. When it is *real* worship, we simply respond. All we can do is fall on our knees in reverent fear before the rightful King.

> Neither Adam nor Eve—nor you nor I—were ever meant to be the center of God's world. We don't have the gravitational pull strong enough to keep everything in its right place.

But Adam's sons and daughters do not kneel. They walk in the counsel of the wicked, stand in the way of sinners, and sit in the seat of scoffers (see Ps. 1:1). While their feet carry them away from their Lord, their hands fashion idols to take His place. This is the irony of idolatry: the gods we create to serve our supposed self-sufficiency undoubtedly become our masters. Eventually, everything we worship in God's place will "enslave us with guilt (if we fail to attain them), or anger (if someone blocks them from us), or fear (if they are threatened), or drivenness (since we must have them)."[5]

Sin, then, is loving something other than God more than God. When we rebel against God, we become less human; we blur His image and distort our God-given reason for existence. Idolaters slowly become the idols they serve: low budget, hollow replicas of the beautiful image they once reflected (see Ps. 115:8). We no longer worship the Lord. In the end, we worship ourselves and the very gifts God gave us in order to worship Him well.

———

IDOLATRY AND CREATIVITY

If sin is loving something more than God, then idolatry is what happens when we apply creativity to this twisted love. Idolatry is the prideful act of adding imagination to our rebellion in order to create something to take God's place in our lives. Creativity and idolatry come as a package deal. Idolatry is what happens when image bearers become image makers with creation's images. It's why creativity so quickly became idolatry's handmaiden after the fall. In the chaos of cosmic treason, those made in the likeness of God fashion replacement gods in their own shattered likeness through their own misplaced creativity.

Creativity for Idols

This toxic equation stains the pages of Christian Scripture. The Old Testament, in fact, is the story of a people struggling with the self-inflicted repercussions of their creative idolatry. Sin, in many ways, is Israel's (and our own) greatest contribution to their redemptive drama. Israel's flight from Egypt is a microcosm of this very struggle. On paper, Israel should be head-over-heels, hands-in-the-air ecstatically in love with God. The Lord just leveled Egypt—the world's greatest superpower and Israel's oppressors—with an onslaught of miracles. He forced them to fill Israel's coffers with their own riches. He plucked His people out of their slavery and put them on the path to a new home.

And with their Egyptian pursuers drowned in the Red Sea behind them and the land of promise on the horizon, Israel stood poised at the base of Mount Sinai waiting for God's next move. But time passed by. Standing turned to sitting while patience turned to impatience. Instead of worshiping the God of their redemption, Israel started to covet the gods of their slavery. So while their mediator, Moses, met the Lord on top of Mount Sinai, Israel bottomed out in idolatry to fashion a god they thought they could manage.

To do so, Israel got creative. They collected all their gold jewelry and gave it to Aaron, Moses's second in command. Aaron melted down their gold and artistically fashioned it with a graving tool into the image of a golden calf. Israel's idolatry continued to manifest itself through creativity. This time they built an altar for their burnt offerings. With their new god in front of their eyes and under their thumb, the people, who were created to multiply God's image in the world, indulged in physical pleasures to worship the god of their own creation. And they went even further, giving their manmade idol credit for their redemption, praising the golden calf as one who "brought [the nation] out of the land of Egypt!" (Ex. 32:4).

The use of creativity for idolatry doesn't end at Sinai either. As the prophet Isaiah details centuries later, Israel continues to pay artists to cast idols, regardless of the gods' ineptitude:

> An idol! A craftsman casts it,
>> and a goldsmith overlays it with gold
>> and casts for it silver chains.
>
> He who is too impoverished for an offering
>> chooses wood that will not rot;
>
> he seeks out a skillful craftsman
>> to set up an idol that will not move. (Isa. 40:19–20)

Creativity fuels Israel's idolatry just as it does ours. This is everyone's temptation: to take God's good gifts and use them for ourselves, our own purposes, and our own twisted desires. Though it may not be idols of gold and wood, in our current culture, we certainly have idols of pixels, harmonies, and design readymade for worship. We keep rectangular idols in our pockets and use our passcode to worship at the altar of our apps whenever there is a break in a conversation—and often when there is not.

Cinemas too can become dark temples, with worshipers gathered together to hear and revere the writer's and director's vision. It's also why some people return to the same film again and again. Some of us are looking for more than entertainment here. We long to find a new hope up in the stars, we want to believe that evil can be overcome by throwing a ring into the fire, and we want to find the perfect world waiting for us with the offer of a new life. When we look at our smartphones or at the movie screen, we are from time to time looking for answers. We want omniscience and salvation. In short, we can use our creativity to create the gods we want rather than the God we need.

Creatives as Idols

As idolaters, we are doing one of two things: we either make a god with our imaginations or make ourselves gods with our imaginations. When we give our creativity divine attributes—autonomy, independence, and sovereignty—we've found a way to compete with God. Worship shifts from golden calves to the artisans who made it. We use creativity and innovation to gain God's privileges without God so we can be god over our world and anyone else willing to worship us.

The Tower of Babel tells us the ancient story of this idolatrous relationship with creativity. In Genesis 11, our ancestors began to build a culture, a city with a tower reaching into the heavens at its center. Their plans were not necessarily evil; they actually reflected humanity's divine call to create and build. But there was a problem—not with the architecture, but with the architects.

The problem lies in our ancestors' motives, what moved them to create. The tower at Babel was an altar to its architects' arrogance. They built it on the precarious foundation of Adam's and Eve's infectious first sin. The now-innate temptation to be like God glazed every brick our ancestors used to build their way into God's heaven on their own terms and in their own power. And in their own words, our ancestors plotted, **"Let us build ourselves a city and a tower with its top in the heavens, and** *let us make a name for ourselves"* **(Gen. 11:4, emphasis added).** They wanted to be God, to show themselves to be self-sufficient creators who could overtake God's glory through creativity. The tower effectively screams, "Look at what we can do on our own! We don't need God, and we certainly don't want Him."

Herein lies the irony, though: Even their attempts at self-sovereignty betray an implicit reliance on God. To make their idolatrous monument, they had to make bricks out of stone and bitumen, which only exist because God made them. It's like many of us with our coffee. We *love* coffee. So much so that we need a thousand different adjectives just to describe it and just as many methods to make it. Coffee is a market built on ingenuity and innovation; yet, when we get to the bottom of our pour over, everything about this whole subculture hinges on a small, dark bean that was given to us by a kind and loving God.

We've said it before and we will say it again: *all* human creativity is derivative. It is never fully original. It is never *ex nihilo*, like God's. Which means everything—even the resources humanity uses for idolatry—is God-given. How easily we forget our place and the place of our creativity. That is sin's toxin. It makes us so ingrown that we can't even recognize the clearest revelations of God and our reliance upon Him. We no longer stop to consider how the stone and bitumen got there to begin with. We just blindly try to use them against the Creator.

Our rebellion against God's original and perfect design twists everything, especially our desires. It's why our ancestors built a tower on the conviction that they no longer needed God, while they still wanted everything He had to offer. Like selfish children who try to lock their parents in their bedroom on Christmas morning, sinners want the gifts without the Giver. They could build their tower into heaven but would tragically find out that heaven is nothing without God. We are living a lie if we believe we can gain God's blessings without Him, because God Himself is the blessing.

The same goes for our creativity. Creativity without God is ultimately self-defeating. It cannot do what it was meant to do, nor can it be what we try to force it to be. Our creativity only "works" in God's plan. He created us to be creative *for His purposes*. But in the fall, we lost the "owner's manual" and tried to make our creativity something that it's not. That's why our creativity only goes so far on its own; that's why it keeps breaking; that's why it can never quite complete us; and that's why it can only hurt us when it's all about ourselves. Creativity wasn't built for your kingdom, it was built for God's. When you unplug your creativity from God, it becomes powerless; and when you plug it into your own idolatry "outlet," it will eventually blow the fuse.

To see this in a different way, let's return to your ship:

It's been some time since you saw the old man, the rundown boatyard, or anything besides seawater for that matter. You've lost track of everything as you stand trapped between the sun burning overhead and its blinding reflection on the waves below. All you have to keep you company is your sail. You remember the first time you saw it there on your front lawn. It was so unique and perfect back then. But now everything is different; it's just a sail. It seems so sterile and utilitarian up there on the mast.

You have an idea. What if you could get closer to your canvas? What if you could see all its glorious detail again? You let go of the ship's stern and start unhinging your sail from its rigging. As you wait to hold it tight in your arms again, you convince yourself that your canvas is the only thing that matters; everything else is worthless in comparison. Even your ship is getting in the way. In your haste, you disconnect your sail from the rigging incorrectly, sending your sail crashing into the ocean rather than into your arms. Panic sets in and, in your sun-scorched delusion, you dive overboard to get back your prized possession. It's too late, though. Your sail is already full of water; it's dragging you straight to the bottom of the sea. Still you won't let go. You

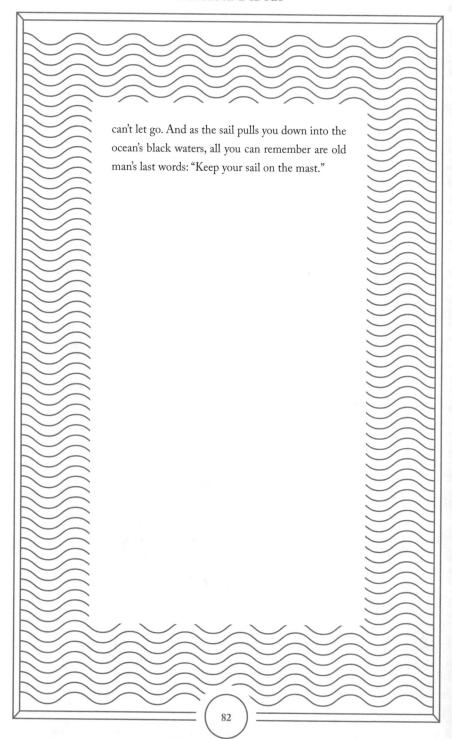

can't let go. And as the sail pulls you down into the ocean's black waters, all you can remember are old man's last words: "Keep your sail on the mast."

Creativity for creativity's sake isn't freedom. It will drown you under the whitecaps of chaos and artistic self-veneration. Creativity, like art, will "always [be] tempted to glory in itself, and nearly, every form of [it] has been used to communicate values that are contrary to Scripture."[6] That is creativity's silver-tongued lie. Our imaginations will always fill the void in our godless world; it will either fashion a new god for us or make us the idol to be worshiped.

IDOLATRY'S CORRUPTION OF CREATIVITY'S PURPOSES

The problem isn't with the creative artifact; the problem is the creative. Or as C. S. Lewis poignantly describes in his classic *The Great Divorce*:

> "No. You're forgetting," said the [heavenly] Spirit [to the Artist who is now a ghost]. "That was not how you began. Light itself was your first love: you loved to paint only as a means of telling about light."

> "Oh, that's ages ago," said the Ghost. "One grows out of that. Of course, you haven't seen my later works. One becomes more and more interested in paint for its own sake."

> "One does, indeed. I also have had to recover from that. It was all a snare. Ink and catgut and paint were necessary

down there, but they are also dangerous stimulants. Every poet and musician and artist, but for Grace, is drawn away from the love of the thing he tells, to love of the telling till, down in Deep Hell, they cannot be interested in God at all but only in what they say about Him. For it doesn't stop at being interested in paint, you know. They sink lower—becoming interested in their own personalities and then in nothing but their own reputations."[7]

Here, Lewis places his scalpel on the center of creativity's cancerous idolatry. Lewis uses a heavenly spirit to educate the ghost of an artist on his misconceptions of his creative task and purpose. The artist has made his work about himself, not about the God who makes the light, which is the fundamental medium behind his painting.

Lewis corrects us by showing us that what we do with our hands and imagine with our minds exposes the real direction of our hearts. And they can go one of two ways: toward God or away from Him. Or as Lewis puts it, toward the love of the Light or away from it.

The Idol of Creativity and God's Glory

Unfortunately, most creatives have exchanged the God of light for the world's limelight. Sure, many begin to write, sing, and paint to glorify the God of words, harmony, and color; but over time, emphasis shifts as the lure of approval and admiration becomes too strong. Creatives become self-enamored and "self-actualized." If it's not serving a divine purpose, our creativity will inevitably become self-serving and ingrown. When our creativity goes unchecked, we will twist it to serve its own ends, which eventually transitions into our own fleeting whims. Or as the prophet Ezekiel sees it, **"Your heart was proud because of your beauty; you corrupted your wisdom for the sake of your splendor"** (Ezek. 28:17).

And when we are left to our own devices, we don't get better. Many creatives do not mature in their beliefs but rather "mature" *beyond* their beliefs. This is often code for "our faith rests fully on ourselves now." God's beauty turns into a stepping-stone on their climb to fame. Like a serial adulterer, they forget and abuse their first love, exchanging His grace and mercy for personal glory and renown. This all just leads to our demise, however. If the works of your hands, the power of your imagination, and the output of your work ethic are just self-serving, then they will all serve to break you—in either this life or the next. Creativity, like all of our idols, can become a treadmill on which, over time, we stumble and lose our footing and grounds for our hope.

We know this because we authors personally have to fight this. The research for this chapter was done mostly in our hearts.

Let this be a gentle reminder to you and to ourselves: our creativity needs our King. He writes the drama and perfects our story. But, in our idolatry, we've become like second-rate actors fighting to write our own second-rate plays, all while we try to forget that we're on the Master's stage in the middle of the opening-night performance. If we would just read God's script, we would realize that the roles He's written for us far surpass our one-dimensional performances with us as the lead. God has written us with intricate beauty and profound depth because His is the master story that makes sense of our individual subplots.

So let us return creativity back to its rightful place, where we create for God's glory and not our own. Remember your first love. Paint the Light.

The Idol of Creativity and the World's Good

Idols are relentless. They won't let go until they have all of who we are. The idol of creativity captures our attention with our own reflection and holds it there until all we can see is ourselves and our imaginative "genius." The world fades into the background, and our neighbors are there only to serve our personal interests. Sure, we want to entertain everyone, we want the audience to love us, and we want them to follow our every move. But it's often for no other reason than to earn their applause and ticket sales.

This is creativity's post-fall hidden agenda: we serve only one master, and when that master is ourselves, we try to manipulate everything else to serve us. This includes our neighbor. We reduce everyone to a retweet or a like in our social media feed. Creatives sit on thrones of their own making, while their followers cast their time and money at their feet.

Over time, though, creatives trade artistic purity for its fringe benefits. As a result, their followers eventually become their leaders; the assumed needs of the audience overtake the creative's initial love. As Flannery O'Connor argues, "Every day we see people who are busy distorting their talents in order to enhance their popularity or to make money that they could do without." But what's worse is when "we see people distorting their talents in the name of God for reasons they think are good."[8]

This particular curse haunts us as much as it does all of modern Christianity. Instead of leading the charge to great art, Christians often chase these same secular paradigms. At best, we make good Xerox copies. This is where *modern Christian creativity* tends to overlap with idolatry. Take much of the music we hear today on Christian radio, for instance. Many of these songs are to real music what idols are to authentic Christianity. Both photocopy the excellence of their source. And it works on us, because we are often too blind to see the real beauty behind the counterfeit.

What we think benefits other Christians as well as the lost, in fact, sometimes does the opposite. I (Ryan) remember being at a nationwide youth conference where the leaders challenged us to make a commitment to replace our secular music with Christian music for thirty days. They promised that if we did, we would never want our old music back. I took the challenge—which meant I spent a lot of money on music at the conference exhibitor's hall (a nice little sales bump for the conference, I'm sure). And when the thirty days were over, I could name you all the secular musical influences the Christian artists replicated, and all I wanted was my old music back. Not because I loved its message but because it was qualitatively better music.

Here is what we know: cookie-cutter creativity doesn't serve our neighbors; it bores them. It pushes them back into the store to find the originals. Today's "boutique" generation has no patience for off-brand creativity. But the point isn't to create to appease the world or to earn their respect anyway. We create because we were made to do so. Turning everything into a gospel tract will not overcome misplaced creativity either. Rather, the best thing we can do is to create beautiful things. As theologian R. C. Sproul put it, "If art is good art, if it is true art, if it is beautiful art, then it is bearing witness to the Author of the good, the true, and the beautiful."[9]

Christians should therefore work the hardest at their craft because they have the best reason to create. Our creativity is sourced directly in the God of beauty and is informed by eternal purposes. That is how we serve our neighbor. When we "understand that people will and should resonate with our work not because it is Christian but because it is good. Above all, Christians should make good art, true art; art unafraid of exploring mystery, portraying evil, and looking for truth wherever it appears."[10] Our creativity finally finds its place when it doesn't just state the good news (a good thing in itself) but gives our neighbors a breathtaking glimpse of that "country we have never yet visited."[11] In a broken world, creatives serve the world by creating beautiful things that will ultimately bridge the fractures. Or as Neil Gaiman succinctly puts it, "When things get tough, this is what you should do: Make good art."[12]

Just remember why you do it. Tend to the divine roots of your creativity. Create for the love of God and the love of neighbor. That is reclaimed creativity; the kind that breaks the world's idolatry and, like a trencadis mosaic, tells a more beautiful story with the broken pieces.

Don't do it for art's sake. Or the artist's. Neither will last. This selfish type of creativity is like a glass of saltwater for those lost in the Sahara. It looks satisfying but only makes us thirstier with every drink we take. Creativity for creativity's sake will never fulfill you because creativity for God's sake and the sake of others is what you were made for.

I did nothing;
the Word did everything.

–MARTIN LUTHER

Change happens not just by giving
the mind new arguments but also
by feeding the imagination new
beauties.

–TIM KELLER

Innovation and creativity actually
can save the world if we let it.

–DONNIE LYGONIS

Life isn't about finding yourself.
Life is about creating yourself.

–GEORGE BERNARD SHAW

4

CREATIVITY
RE-CREATED

*WHAT JESUS
HAS TO DO WITH YOUR CREATIVITY*

No company wields its creativity to save the world more than Facebook.

In fact, Facebook's creator and CEO, Mark Zuckerberg, laid out his very own salvation plan of sorts in a nearly 6,000-word epistle in early 2017. His manifesto leads with a simple and direct question: "Are we building the world we want?"

This question reverberates throughout the rest of the letter, as well as every corner of his social network. It's also the driving force behind Zuckerberg's all-consuming utopian vision that he hopes his company can help usher in.

According to Facebook, our world stands at the threshold of excellence. We are close to being something great, something perfect; but we are not quite where Zuckerberg wants us to be. We need help, and Facebook can—and now wants—to prop open paradise's doors digitally for us. As Zuckerberg proposes,

> Today we are close to taking our next step. Our greatest opportunities are now global—like spreading prosperity and freedom, promoting peace and understanding, lifting people out of poverty, and accelerating science. Our greatest challenges also need global responses—like ending terrorism, fighting climate change, and preventing pandemics. Progress now requires humanity coming together not just as cities or nations, but also as a global community.[1]

Now for the sales pitch:

> Facebook stands for bringing us closer together and building a global community. . . . In times like these, the most important thing we at Facebook can do is develop the social infrastructure to give people the power to build a global community that works for all of us.[2]

Zuckerberg thinks "this global community" is the best option for the better world he imagines. At times, his vision even sounds redemptive and it runs so deep, it's completely overhauled Facebook's central mission. Speaking to an audience of his favorite digital "communities," Zuckerberg announced that Facebook's new purpose was to "give people the power to build community and bring the world closer together." "Bringing the world together" allows the restorative power of personal (read digital) connection to autocorrect our wayward world. As the CEO puts it,

> Communities give us that sense that we are part of something bigger than ourselves, that we are not alone, that we have something better ahead to work for. We all get meaning from our communities. . . . [T]hey give us the strength to expand our horizons and care about broader issues.[3]

According to Zuckerberg, the global community can actually save you. Community is the foremost way to "ending poverty, curing disease, stopping climate change, spreading freedom and tolerance, stopping terrorism."[4] We can achieve utopia just by pushing the world closer together.

At least that's what it says on Facebook.

When you pull back the rhetorical curtain, however, we find the social network's real savior. It's not just *a* global community; it is *the* global community *Facebook* offers you. The one digitally curated for your networking pleasure. Facebook has read your online prayers and sits poised to answer them. They make straight the way to a better digital world. It's why Facebook covenants, with each of its users (one in four people worldwide), to make you your very own personal, infinite, social infrastructure creatively adapted "for supporting us, for keeping us safe, for informing us, for civic engagement, and for inclusion of all."[5]

———

WHAT CHRIST MEANS FOR CREATIVITY

The social network's plan to save you through its virtual creativity, however, has a fatal flaw—as do all salvation plans outside of Christ. Zuckerberg never asks the more basic question assumed in these utopian ambitions. The question haunting Facebook's new ideal (digital) world is simply: Why does the world need Facebook's help in the first place?

Ironically, Zuckerberg's answer turns out to be the very "salvation" he offers us through Facebook. Community can't make the world a better place, because communities are made up of those who broke the world with their sin in the first place. The problem with the world—the very reason the world isn't the way any of us, including Zuckerberg, want it to be—is you and me.

In the end, Facebook's creative promise of salvation-through-community turns out to be a dead end rather than a digital highway to paradise. Lurking behind this well-dressed sentiment is a dangerous naïveté about the human heart. Facebook's "community complex" is just a collection of overidealized assumptions about our humanity.[6] Building redemption on communities of sinners united in their creativity is like building a bomb shelter out of activated bombs.[7] To avoid the shrapnel of our own making, we need a better conception of the human heart and our creative acts.[8]

It boils down to this: Facebook gets the diagnosis partially right. Our world *does* need fixing. Where Facebook goes wrong—where we all go wrong—is thinking that *we* can fix it on our own terms in our own power or through our own creativity. Sinners can't save sinners, no matter how creative they are. We cannot save the world, and simply establishing online communities doesn't change this. In fact, our efforts tend to magnify our problems, intensify personal sins, and twist our creativity into systemic evil (see Gen. 11:1–9).

Yet we keep asking the world to save us from the world. It's like the frantic logic of two men clawing and scraping their way over each other as they freefall in tandem off a sixty-seven-story building. Regardless of who hits first, both return to dust. When left to ourselves, our end is inevitable. We can't stop falling and we can't outrun the ground. Something—or better yet, *someone*—else must stop our fall.

This is why Christ Jesus came into the world. He who was outside of our freefall traded places with us to save us from the imminent demise of our sin. The Creator creatively became the created to re-create His creation.

This is how He did it.

The Re-Creator Enters His Creation

The Gospels start with the unexpected: God became man. The Word of God took on flesh. The author of our faith wrote *Himself* into His own story. This means the fully divine Son of God became fully human without compromising His divinity. In the Lord's wise and perfect plan, God the Son also became the Son of Man. In doing so, the second person of the Trinity did not lose, set aside, or confuse His divinity. Rather, He took on the mental, emotional, volitional, and bodily nature of humanity. Jesus, **"according to the flesh, is the Christ"** and simultaneously **"God over all, blessed forever" (Rom. 9:5).** The incarnation is how the **"Lord of Glory"** (divine nature) can, at the same time, be the **"crucified"** (human nature) One **(1 Cor. 2:8).** Jesus Christ entered our broken world as the God-Man in order to humble Himself **"by becoming obedient to the point of death, even death on a cross" (Phil. 2:8).** This is where God's beautiful re-creative work recklessly breaks into your world.

The Re-Creator Ministers to His Creation

Re-creation defines not only Christ's appearing, but also His ministry. In fact, His public ministry prepares us for His cross work and interprets it for us. And the summary of His teachings is heard in His call for us to follow Him. Christ commands us to replicate His life of service and self-sacrifice. His public ministry is how He shows, teaches, offers, pictures, speaks, preaches, and demonstrates His re-creative work before the world's watching eyes so that we might become like Him (1 John 3:2).

> *The Creator creatively became the created to re-create His creation.*

Christ's call to follow Him is a call to reimagine humanity. Christ enters His global theater to rewrite and reenact the human drama.[9] We see this most clearly when Christ enters the wilderness to face Satan's temptation. This prelude to His public ministry isn't just another stock description of His moral perfection. Rather, it's a glorious portrait of His reversing Adam's—and thereby humanity's—slavery to sin. Jesus casts Himself as the better Adam, the one standing on the world's stage to build a better kingdom out of the ruins of the first Adam's.

When Jesus steps out of the Jordan's baptismal waters, He marches directly into the Judean wilderness to fast and prepare for the ministry set out before Him. Starved for forty days in the wasteland, Jesus—though without sin—experiences the bitter consequences of Adam's curse firsthand. And, as if right on cue, Satan takes center stage at Christ's weakest point to twist his knife into this new Adam by twisting truth into lies and lies into truth.

This time the devil has home-field advantage. Christ fights temptation not in the perfect garden but in the curse-scorched wilderness. He faces Satan not as one filled and satisfied with the provisions of paradise but as the emaciated, sallow, and starving servant cast out in exile. The devil stays with the same playbook; no need to change a "winning" strategy, right? Satan offers Christ the same promises He made to Adam and Eve in Eden. The tempter tempts Jesus with what is **"good for food . . . a delight to the eyes, and . . . desired to make one wise" (Gen. 3:6).** The devil entices the Son to feed His empty stomach by turning stones into bread (Matt. 4:3–4). To His sun-weary eyes, he offers the Messiah all the world's kingdoms in all their worldly beauty (Matt. 4:8–10). And to His new status of humility, Satan entices Jesus with the prideful possibility of manipulating His Father with the Father's own promises (Matt. 4:5–7).

In three acts, the garden's first temptation was replayed on the barren stage of the wilderness with crueler severity and crushing potency. Yet Jesus did not give in. He pushed Satan's enticements back with God's Word. In His humanity, Christ overcame the human fight against the flesh, beauty, and pride, cutting a path through sin and temptation for His followers to follow Him. Where the first Adam fell, the better Adam stood His ground; where the first Adam opened the doors to death, the better Adam opened the doors to eternal life; and where the first Adam forced us out of the garden, the better Adam made a way back into paradise. That is why He calls us to follow Him. When we do, He leads us out of the wasteland back into God's better promises.

The Re-Creator Restores His Creation

For Christ, this road out of the wilderness led to a forsaken hill outside of Jerusalem. Jesus' re-creative work finds its thorn-crowning achievement in the crimson drops pooled at the foot of a Roman cross. But His death is no ordinary death. It is a servant's death; it is a vicarious death. Christ "came not to be served but to serve" (Mark 10:45, emphasis added). And how does the Son of God serve those who reject, oppose, mock, and despise Him? By doing the unimaginable. He dies for them. He dies to buy them back, pay their ransom, and make them alive again. All by dying in their place. You see, "while we were still sinners, Christ died *for* us" (Rom. 5:8); He was offered up as a sacrifice "to *bear the sins of many*" (Heb. 9:28). He "died *for the ungodly*" (Rom. 5:6, all emphases added).

For sinners like *you*. For sinners like *us*.

His road out of the wilderness, though, didn't end on the cross. No, it was finished in an empty tomb. Though our sins killed the Author of our faith, the Father wrote Him back to life, raising Him from the dead (Acts 3:15). Death cannot hold Jesus, because Christ has no sin for death to grip (1 Peter 2:22). He didn't succumb to temptation in the wilderness, nor outside the wilderness, either.

Christ's death and resurrection, therefore, didn't pay the wages for His own sin, but, in grace and by His blood, He paid for ours. God makes those who were once dead in sin alive together with Christ. By putting faith in Jesus—the one God raised from the dead—you too can be raised with Him. We have everything when we have Christ: because He is without sin, He can take away our sins (1 John 3:5); because He rises from the dead, we too can have a resurrected life.

———

THE CREATIVE WORK OF CHRIST

This may help us better understand our faith, but what does it have to do with our creativity? Is the gospel—the life, death, and resurrection of Christ—actually something we can build our creative lives on? Or do they stand in opposition to one another?

To know salvation is to know God's imagination. Creativity is woven into the whole fabric of the gospel. Christ uses redemptive creativity to re-create His creation. He turns enemies into sons and daughters. He gives the blind sight, the thirsty everlasting water, the broken healing, and the dead new life. The gospel, God's work of re-creation in us, is the greatest act of redemptive creativity.

The Creative Work of Christ's Incarnation

Take the incarnation. To love the incarnation is to love the Creator's transcendent creativity. God's imaginative genius was on full display in the Bethlehem manger, where Jesus—the God over all creation—filled the night sky that He created with His cries and the world He made with His glory. In the incarnation, God creatively unites majesty with meekness in the Lord *over* history and, now, *in* history. We love these striking juxtapositions of God's incarnational design because it displays the depths of God's creative love for us—a love so unrelenting that neither sin, nor time, nor space, nor humanity can stop it.

The creative impulse that fuels the incarnation doesn't wait for the first chapter of Matthew. Page 1 of the Old Testament tells us that God has put His image in His world since the beginning of creation. As we saw in chapter 2, God makes humanity to be His image bearers and represent Him in the cosmos He spoke into existence. Even after the fall, God doesn't stop His creative self-revelation as we might think. He continues to picture Himself in humanity—though now fractured through sin. But on the other side of Adam's sin, God also builds a whole creative catalog of character communication in the symbols, events, and institutions that line the pages of the Old Testament to lead us to Christ in the New.

One of the most brilliant examples of God's creative fore-shadowing in the Old Testament is the tabernacle. Here, God reveals His nature through a tentlike structure, and He uses an artist to accomplish this revelation. Enter Bezalel, the tabernacle's chief craftsman whom the Lord Himself fills with the Spirit to build a sanctuary that could hold God's beauty (see Ex. 35:30–35). Every creative detail of the tabernacle is God-centered and God-commanded. From the curtain to the frames, from the bars of acacia wood to the Ark of the Covenant, from the table of presence to the veil, and from the altars of sacrifice to its overall architectural design, each element tells us who God is and that He has come to prepare a way out of exile and back into His presence. In the tabernacle, God draws near to His people so that they could draw near to Him.

This is the same thing He does in Christ, but better. What the Old Testament imaged, the New Testament incarnates. The tabernacle creatively promises what Jesus creatively completes. The Old Testament sanctuary's beauty pushes our minds forward to God's greatest image: His Son, Jesus Christ, who, in becoming flesh, tabernacled among us (see John 1:14).[10]

The incarnation is like the opening of an art gallery, filled not just with the artist's work but, more importantly, with the Artist Himself.

This is why Paul describes Jesus Christ as "the image of the invisible

God" (Col 1:15). The Greek term for "image" in this passage is where we get our word *icon*. Jesus, then, is the creative one who, in the incarnation, pictures God in all His glory to the world He has come to save. Christ is the manifestation of God and the portrait of God's glory, beauty, and even creativity.

The Creative Work of Christ's Ministry

God's creativity extends from Christ's appearing into Christ's public ministry as well. Everything Christ does seeks to reimage us. His public ministry is where His work to repair the image of God in all of us begins. Like a sculptor, He uses His words to conform us to His own image (Rom. 8:29), to fashion us from men and women of dust into men and women of heaven (1 Cor. 15:49), and to clothe us in His righteousness (Eph. 4:24). He is the *model* of restored humanity, the *messenger* who teaches us what our restoration entails, and the *means* through which we are restored to God. Our journey back to true humanity begins with His call to take up our cross and follow Him.

Jesus' public ministry hinges on His teaching, which is where the light of God's creativity shines through brightly. Christ doesn't minister in His world like we think He should. He certainly wasn't what His people were expecting their messiah to be. He doesn't talk like a seminary professor and He doesn't sound like any other preacher you've heard. He sounds more like a storyteller, a sage, or a poet. He constantly replaces the propositions and imperatives of the Pharisees with the imaginative language of similes, analogies, metaphors, and parables to build the kingdom of heaven in the minds *and hearts* of His audience. To make the Father known and to help the world understand His love, Christ paints the world with powerful images and imaginative pictures. It's why salvation is about being "born again." It's why He "ransoms" sinners through the cross. It's why Christ is our Good Shepherd, the way, the truth, the life, the Light of the World and on and on it goes.[11] These pictures hang on the walls of our consciousness; they are indelible representations that show us what Christ has done and how we should feel about it. Christ talks in images to capture us and lead us out of the wilderness with Him.

Creativity helps the infinite God show and tell His finite creations who He is and how much He loves them. This is one of the basic reasons for our creativity in the first place. Creativity is a common language that God instills in us so we may know and experience Him in full. We were made to crave truth from all angles. And in His creative words and teaching, Christ pushes these very buttons He put in us. He communicates through the full spectrum of our emotions and sensory experience to confront us with a love so amazing, so divine that it demands our soul, our life, our all. [12]

The Creative Work of Christ's Redemption

The incarnation is for our redemption. Christ's public ministry is for our redemption. And our redemption is for our re-creation. Jesus' work on the cross is much more than a sterile act of cosmic legislation; it is a beautiful act of re-imagination. The death and resurrection of

Christ remakes us and redesigns us. This is why we are commanded to put on the new self, created after the likeness of God (Eph. 4:24). The cross is one of the greatest expressions of creativity the world has ever seen, and Jesus is the world's transcendent creative. Yes, Christ redeems us from our sins, but His redemption accomplishes so much more. Christ saves the world by redesigning the world (see Rom. 8:22–24); Christ's death and resurrection triumphs over the world's poisonous powers and precarious patterns; He topples sin's stronghold and breaks the doors off death's dungeon; and in its place, He creates a reimagined right-side-up-again kingdom defined by His glorious beauty.

Jesus not only re-creates us but also uses art to explain how He will accomplish this re-creation. In John 3, Christ links His coming death to God's judgment in Numbers 21, where God used snakes to punish Israel for her obstinate heart in the wilderness. That ancient punishment was quick and severe, but so was God's mercy. To afford the Israelites grace, God commanded Moses to fashion the form of a snake in bronze. He was then to fasten it to His staff and hold it high so that those bitten by the snakes could look upon it and live. Confronted with the poison of their sin, Israel repented, obeyed God's command, and found God's mercy by looking to Moses's artwork. By staring directly into the eyes of the bronze serpent, Israel was forced to look unflinchingly into the dark consequences of their rebellion in order to find their salvation.

Jesus announces that, like the bronze serpent lifted up in the wilderness, He too would be lifted up—not on Moses's staff, but on a Roman cross. In making this connection, Jesus deepens our understanding of God's love and grace for us. Moses's creative work wasn't just for Israel; His art foretold the disturbing brilliance of Christ's work on the cross. But where Moses's art brought Israel face to face with her sin, Christ's death went further. It brings us face to face with God's atoning provision. Israel looked at the snake to be saved; Christians look at their God. The bronze snake showed Israel that God would save His people through judgment; Jesus shows us that God saves His people by taking their judgment upon Himself. At the cross, the judge becomes the judged. The snake that bites becomes the snake that is bit. Christ takes our poison by drinking our poison. The sinless becomes our sin (2 Cor. 5:21).[13]

This is the gospel, the most strikingly creative drama ever conceived. Who would have ever cast the God of the universe into the role of the servant who suffers on behalf of His enemies? No one except the Author and Artist of the Christian faith. And so He did. He sent Christ Jesus, who was the very form of God and who emptied Himself by being born in the likeness of man to die in our place (Phil. 2:6–8). The one in whom the fullness of God was pleased to dwell reconciles the world to God by making peace through the blood on the cross (Col. 1:19–20). This is what distinguishes Christianity from every other religion in the world: the transcendent one becomes the immanent one; the author writes Himself into His own story to re-create the cosmos through redemptive creativity by standing in the theater of His creation.

Jesus and My Creativity

Sure, this is great news. But what does any of this have to do with your creativity in your right-here-right-now world? What does Jesus have to do with your art, music, words, or any other creative medium you use to fill the world with beauty? Our simple answer: everything.

But to avoid oversimplification, let us explain. God doesn't want your art. He wants *you*—all of you. And when He has all of you, He has your art—the motivation behind it and the purposes for it as well. Christ cares about your creativity because He cares about creatives. He cares enough to die for you and, as a result, to die for your creative work. This means that Christ doesn't need your creativity. He *wants* all of you, which includes the gifts He has given you for His glory. Just as Christ doesn't redeem just a few parts of you, neither does He seek to transform everything but your creativity. He wants to make all of you like Him in every way.

> We effectively say, "Lord, take everything, but just let me have my creativity. You can have me on Sundays but not during the week. You can have me in the church's sanctuary, but let me have my studio."

We suspect—actually, we know personally—that this is the creative's greatest stumbling block when it comes to Christianity. We'd like to alter the covenant with God. We want to edit our contract with Him, without Him knowing. We effectively say, "Lord, take everything, but just let me have my creativity. I want to use this to make a name for myself, provide for my family, and [insert your favorite hyper-spiritualized justification here]. You can have me on Sundays but not during the week. You can have me in the church's sanctuary, but let me have my studio."

Our spiritual gift is compartmentalization. But here is the problem: If Christ isn't finally and fully the Lord over all of us, then He isn't our Lord at all. If God doesn't rule over our creativity, then our creativity has become our God (see chapter 3). When this is the case, we've allowed something outside Christ's reign to reign over us.[14] You cannot serve both God and creativity.

Creatives usually don't struggle with the need for salvation; they struggle with where to find it and how to stay there. And if you aren't vigilant, your worship will always recalibrate around your gifts. But don't take our word for it; you can hear it in these artists' own voices:

> Art should cause violence to be set aside and it is only art that can accomplish this.[15] (Leo Tolstoy)

> The point of being an artist is that you may live. . . . The object of art is not to make salable pictures. It is to save yourself.[16] (Sherwood Anderson)

> Painting completed my life.[17] (Frida Kahlo)

> I was born this way, born to make art, to make hip hop. And I think I'm just one of the people who had the courage to stay with my born identity. Hip hop keeps me true to myself, keeps me human.[18] (KRS One)

Art Saves Lives. (A bumper sticker on the Subaru in front of us in Portland traffic)

What's the common refrain? Our art and our creativity will save us. But it never has and never will. There is one more though that rings true:

Beauty will save the world.[19] (Fyodor Dostoevsky)

When we tie beauty to its divine source, Dostoevsky is right. And when you find this utmost beauty in the blood-soaked Lamb who washes you white as snow, it destroys the need to separate our creativity from His cross.

At a practical level, this doesn't mean that you have to paint Jesus into every painting or add fifteen "alleluias" behind every chorus on your album. But it does mean that you let the Lord rule and reign over every canvas and every chord progression. More importantly, the Lord needs to reign over the heart from which your creativity springs.

God has given you a spectrum of creativity for you to use to rejoice in and to create with and to worship Him through. Following Christ means that you are now open in new ways to the diversity and depth of creation. So, preach common grace with your painting. Illuminate God's special revelation with your calligraphy. Sing hymns to our pains and sufferings. Write poems that split the heart open, not just the heavens.

Now, many will say, "But creativity, especially modern creativity, is rebellious, shocking, truth-seeking rather than truth-declaring. It's supposed to be in-your-face, overwhelming, shouting-at-the-top-of-its-lungs-to-get-your-attention-and-break-you-from-the-slavery-of-this-world type of creativity. And Christianity is part of the slavery creativity has to fight. The gospel is the exact opposite of creativity. It's 'opium for the masses,' the chains of creativity, not the key. And now you're telling me that it's supposed to unlock my creativity and it's the fuel for my art? No way, and no thank you."

To which we reply: We get it. We've been there. We've felt what you likely feel. But we were behind enemy lines. Let us be honest with you: If you think Christianity and creativity are at odds, your problem isn't with Jesus; it's with what you think Christianity is. What if you've got it all wrong? What if your chains aren't Christianity but the popular claims of the world? What if you're actually enslaved to your creativity? And what if we told you that the thing you love about your creativity—that glimmer of transcendence that captivates you—is actually a distant reflection of the God of Scripture reflected in your image bearing? Why worship the result when you can have the cause? Why try to drink from a dry riverbed when God has shown you the river's wellspring? Why warm yourself with a spark when Christ offers you a fire?

We've all had this backwards at one point or another. That's why we've written this book. We want you to see that the gospel—the real, true gospel—is the greatest act of creative rebellion the world has ever seen. It is the cry of war against the enemy who has enslaved you, dulled your senses, and hijacked your creativity. Those in the Redeemer's cause push back the darkness with all they have, with their restored and reinvigorated creativity. Take up your creativity and follow Him. Be free and fight for a real freedom to declare His beauty, and create beauty that will last—forever.

This can happen when the Creator of the world is yours and you are His. In His re-creation, your creativity finds true freedom to explore the full range of the human experience—*and now you're invited to know the divine One.* The gospel does not limit you; it frees you from fear and idolatry. Christ's lordship doesn't undercut your creativity; it gives it a reason, hope, future, and borderless kingdom to explore. The One who created your senses—the anthropological instruments for your creativity—is the One who has come to redeem them. He draws near so that you and your creativity may truly **"be set free from its bondage to corruption and obtain the freedom of the glory of the [creative] children of God" (Rom. 8:21).**[20]

> *The gospel does not limit you; it frees you from fear and idolatry.*

So remember, Christ sets your creativity free. Don't submit your creativity to slavery again (see Gal. 5:1), and don't use this freedom as an opportunity for sin (see Gal. 5:13). Work hard. Be disciplined. Exercise your gifts. Trust in your re-Creator.

Your fight against the ocean helps you see this from a different perspective:

Your sail keeps pulling you deeper into the sea's darkness.

But just as you think you're closing your eyes for the last time, you feel a shift in direction. Your sail is pulling you toward the surface, not the seafloor. Light begins to break above into the dark waters. As you near the surface, you see a pair of hands pulling your sail toward your ship. When he sees you, the same hands pull you out of the ocean and back on deck.

As you cough to clear the water from your lungs, the young man addresses you: "I am the Shipbuilder, the Sailmaker, and the ocean's Architect. I have made everything around you and have ordered it for good purposes. Your sail works only when you use it the way I made it to be used. Keep your sail on the mast and you will find what you are looking for." He then leans over the bow and pulls what was left of your sail aboard your ship.

"Will you follow this command?" he asks when he's done. You squeak out a faint yes. "Will you let me make your sail what I intended it to be?" You want to quibble because you love your old sail, but with the saltwater still stinging your lungs, you're beginning to recognize how reckless you've been. So you timidly nod in affirmation.

The Sailmaker makes quick work of the restoration. He wrings out the saltwater and repairs the sail's tatters and tears from your seaborne struggle. Then he does something unexpected. He begins to unfold your sail at the corners. It expands in size and beauty in ways you never imagined. As he attached your enhanced sail to the old mast, he whispered something inaudible into the wood and your ship grows until it matches the sail's new dimensions.

Your rescuer has done the impossible. He has made the most beautiful design you've ever known, somehow *more* beautiful. Something new sits at the center of your sail, something that seems to be the source of the sail's new grandeur. You recognize it to be an insignia of some sort, a coat of arms perhaps, but with arrows and an unreadable script. The Sailmaker leans in and explains, "Your sail bears my seal and holds my compass now. With it, you are free to sail anywhere in my seas and explore everything under my sun. Just remember whose sail this is, whose ship you captain, and whose insignia you sail under. Remember your commitments to me as I will always remember my commitments to you. Go now and sail under my name and keep my sail on my mast."

WHY YOUR CREATIVITY MATTERS
TO CHRIST

Our creativity needs Jesus. He redeems all of who we are and realigns our creativity in the process. At the root of His redemptive creativity is the restoration of purpose. When we answer the *why* of creativity selfishly, we get into trouble. But when we let God answer it, our creativity is put in its right place. Christ reframes all of our existence, including our creativity, when He states with elegant simplicity, **"You shall love the Lord your God with all your heart and with all your soul and with all your strength and with all your mind, and your neighbor as yourself" (Luke 10:27).** Christ's greatest commandment teaches us how our creativity can make sense again. It shows us that we no longer have to assume its goodness. It unites our creativity to the source of transcendence that we're all seeking in every piece of art.[21] In short, the gospel makes our creativity a chorus of God's glory and a song sung for the world.

Creativity and His Glory

Christ does not stand against your creativity, but He does stand over it. Your creativity was and will always be an instrument of worship. The gospel re-creates all of you so that every part of you, including your creativity, is from Christ, through Christ, and to Christ. The gospel retunes your creativity to sing His grace. It re-creates your creativity so that it can do what *He* made it to do—to bring God glory, forever.

In this light, creativity is like kintsugi, the Japanese art that transforms broken ceramics into beautiful works of re-creativity. The key to this process is a special lacquer derived from gold, silver, or platinum powder that the artist uses to adhere the pieces together. Running through the pottery is the glittering evidence of the pottery's past and the promise of its future. The gold and silver lines stand out against the muted tones of the earthenware like our own scars tell the tales of our lives.

All creativity from a Christian perspective, then, is like kintsugi in form. This art isn't really about the pottery, or the piece's remade utility; it is about *restoration*. It's about the *fractures*. All you see when you look at one of these pieces are the gold and silver threads rejoining the once-shattered pottery back together. Its beauty is in the lacquer's ability to transform what was broken into something more beautiful than the original.

The gospel does the same to our lives and creativity. Where we're fractured, the Lord pieces us back together through Christ and seals us with His Spirit. And where we've broken our creativity into millions of little idols, God pulls it all back together for those who love Him.

For the creative, this means that you find beauty in the places where God has healed you and transformed your creativity. It means that you allow God to weave His beautiful restoration into every one of your creative acts. Let the One who has healed your fractures get the glory of your life and your life's work. Put the golden and silver threads of God's providence on display. Show how God weaves your fractured life and art back together and holds it in place. When you do, the world will mostly see His glory, but you shouldn't mind. Your eyes will be captured by it, too.

Creativity and the Good of the World

Creativity, like love, is not a selfish act. Remember, it has both a vertical and horizontal orientation, for God and for neighbor. Our creativity is at its best when it lifts our eyes to transcendence and forces the world to wrestle with its Creator. "The trumpet of imagination," as G. K. Chesterton says, "is like the trumpet of the Resurrection, it calls the dead out of their graves."[22] Your creativity is bigger than you—it exists for God and for others.[23]

For creatives, this means we love our neighbor practically in creative ways. The gospel turns our creativity into a kaleidoscope. Our lives and creative work are the colored glass that the Lord shapes and patterns for the world to see through the other end. All we have to do is hand the kaleidoscope to our neighbor. But we have to remind them that—just like the kaleidoscope—the full spectrum of your creativity is seen only when it's held up to the Light.

Loving the world also means we let our creativity encourage obedience to Christ. "Creativity for obedience" sounds like a contradiction, but it's actually not. Obedience isn't the opposite of freedom. Captivity is. Obedience is a choice. Captivity isn't. The problem with submission is not the act itself but to whom you submit yourself. Does this one hold the keys to your prison or the keys to a kingdom? This is one of the greatest deceptions of our generation: that freedom is doing whatever you want whenever you want, and that it is free of discipline, obedience, and submission. Yet everything we cherish and build our hopes on demands these things. You don't find love in marriage without mutual submission to the other's good. You don't find joy in your creativity without being disciplined in your craft. You can't find wisdom in this world outside of obedience. Your life literally depends on it. That is why you stop at red lights.

Every time you run from obedience, you run back into captivity. The gospel, though, obliterates this. And if the gospel fills your creativity, then your creativity will assault this worldview, too. This is real freedom and the way your creativity serves the world at large. Your life and creative work become keys to the prison doors of the world's lies and idolatry.

What does loving our neighbor through our creativity look like practically? Does it turn our creativity into some kind of artsy gospel tract that paints, sings, writes, or somehow tells others about Jesus in new and inventive ways?

It depends.

It can.

But it doesn't have to.

Before we answer, though, we have one question for you: Why does the idea of "art as evangelism" turn your stomach? Maybe it doesn't. But if it does, you may want to think harder about the reasons.

With that said, we think the guiding principle is this: creative freedom, enlivened by the gospel, is not about doing whatever you want but about wanting to do what God made you to do. Which means you have options, but you also need the wisdom, discernment, and counsel from God fearers—not only creatives—to help you assess your gifts and your direction.

Wanting to make a film doesn't mean you should make a film. Just like enjoying preaching doesn't mean you should be a preacher. It may mean you are the critic who gets inside and behind the film's meaning. Or maybe the teacher who uses the film to apply God's truth. Maybe you have the gift-set to fill a high-end Manhattan gallery with your painting. Or it may mean that you design book covers, even Christian book covers. But it could also mean that you create and design gospel tracts that beautifully and clearly present the good news of Jesus Christ. Each of these examples articulates God's love to our neighbor.

If you are the Lord's, then creativity cannot help but speak His name. Sometimes it will speak between the lines, and others on the title page.

In the end, follow the Lord's example. God presents His glory in both general and special creative acts. They both declare His glory and demonstrate aspects of His nature—but He doesn't limit Himself to one genre or mode. Everything He does in His world He does for His glory and our good. It flows out of Him. This is the model for your creativity. It should be a freeing one. Not every creative project has to be a specific testimony to God's glory. Some can be general, others can be specific. The rule that should guide your creativity, then, is this: Let everything you create be for God's glory and for the world's good. But the ways you can do this are unlimited, as long as they are tethered to God's promises.

So sing hymns. Speak propositions. Write stories. Sing the Psalms. Score new songs. Explore human complexities. But do so in a way that you cannot run fast enough to lay your art at the foot of God's throne.

Music is the exaltation of the mind derived
from things eternal, bursting forth in
sound.

–THOMAS AQUINAS

To me, the arts are handiwork that
continually whisper, "There's more to life
than what you see."

–MIKE COSPER

Everyone must leave something behind
when he dies, my grandfather said. A child
or a book or a painting or a house or a wall
built or a pair of shoes made. Or a garden
planted. Something your hand touched
some way so your soul has somewhere to go
when you die, and when people look at that
tree or that flower you planted, you're there.

–RAY BRADBURY

Norman: "My father was very sure about
certain matters pertaining to the universe.
To him, all good things—trout as well as
eternal salvation—came by grace. And
grace comes by art. And art does not
come easy."

–A RIVER RUNS THROUGH IT

5

THE CRESCENDO
OF CREATIVITY

*WHAT THE NEW CREATION
HAS TO DO WITH YOUR CREATIVITY*

N o creative company capitalizes on the concept of
paradise quite like the Walt Disney Company.

Walt Disney was a dreamer who set out to fill the
world with enchantment, hope, and happiness. And the world loved
his dream. His company grew and flourished, and with it, so did his
desire to create a better, more joyful world. Nothing seemed to slow
his can-do attitude or hope-building machine of a company. The
world seemed to want everything that came from his imagination.

Disney's dream was big. He didn't want to just revolutionize the
way we watch movies; he wanted to change our whole lives. Which
is why he set out to transfer his brand of magic from the celluloid
world of film into the physical world of theme parks. He wanted to
create a place of joy where all your favorite characters and memories

weren't stuck on a screen but could walk down the street with you and could give you a hug.

In the summer of 1955, Disney built his own heaven on earth, a park he called Disneyland. In just a few years, he was able to turn some dusty orange groves into "The Happiest Place on Earth," where kids and families were able to see his dreams come alive and find inspiration for their own imagination along the way.

And this dream was contagious. Heaven couldn't be contained to California. No, Disney wanted to bookend all of America and then fill the world with his dream. So in 1971, a few years after Walt Disney's death, his company completed the Magic Kingdom. Just like that, "The Most Magical Place on Earth" turned out to be forty-eight square miles of Florida swampland, and admission came with a ticket price.

In less than twenty years, Disney gave us his vision of a better world, one of "imagination, hopes, and dreams," a "timeless land of enchantment, [where] the age of chivalry, magic, and make-believe are reborn—and fairy tales come true."[1] He took the perfect memories of his past and tied them to the hopes of the future. That is why when you walk into Disneyland, you walk into "the Missouri of [Walt's] childhood," which "was theoretically the inspiration for Main Street, U.S.A., though only in its halcyon summer-vacation moments and stripped of any dismal memories: no blizzards, no doctor's office, and no schoolhouse. Almost no one has a dismal experience in Walt Disney's America, as a matter of fact—at least not that Walt noticed."[2]

And when you turn off Main Street into Fantasyland, "you leave today and enter the world, of yesterday, tomorrow, and fantasy." He dedicated this new world to the "young and the young-at-heart— to those who believe that when you wish upon a star your dreams do come true." This heaven-is-right-around-the-corner vision also built the foundation for Disney World's EPCOT Center (a.k.a. Experimental Living Center of Tomorrow), finished in 1982. Disney used the future to his advantage because he wasn't just interested in entertaining his audience. He wanted "to show America how it ought to live," which, in his parks, his vision of paradise, "was given free rein in a corporate-sponsored vision of the perfect life awaiting us in the future."[3]

Disney parks assault your senses with magic and perfection so you can trade in your humdrum life for a better one. Every experience is new and overwhelming. There you can stand face-to-face with your imagination's greatest heroes, and you can jump into your favorite spaceship for a quick ride. It's why countless people give their lives to Disney's vision, spending much of their free time at Disney World or getting ready for their next trip. And it's why the sky seems a bit grayer when you leave Disney and why so many wish their lives were a bit more the way Walt imagined it.

Disney takes our traditions, hopes, happiness, and assumptions, and creatively forges a place where our imaginations can run free while our problems fade away. Disney has capitalized on our deep desire to forget our troubles and follow our dreams again. It's why the six-year-old walking through Disneyland's gates for the first time turns to her parents and asks, "Is this what Heaven is like?" And it's why the parents just smile and say "almost."[4] This is exactly what Walt Disney wanted. He wanted Mickey, Minnie, Donald, and Pluto to wipe away every tear from your eyes, and with every ride, meal, show, and experience to make your joy complete.

The Walt Disney Company wants to give you heaven. And in many ways, it delivers.

At least until you have to leave or until you get your credit card statement. Or until your kid gets the flu. Or until you realize how long you've been standing in line.

Disney can push the world back for only so long. The gates are high, but not high enough to keep the world out. Problems, tears, and struggles rush into Disney's utopia because sinners like you and us fill, work in, and create the parks. Disney cannot keep the ancient serpent outside its kingdom. Sin and death don't need a ticket to enter the happiest place on earth. The curse is everywhere, regardless of how many times you paint the façade or how quickly you pick up the litter.

Embedded in every park, movie, stuffed animal, and sing along microphone that bears Disney's name are two truths: like Disney himself, we all want, need, and hope for a better world; and no matter how creative or imaginative we are, none of us can make that world on our own.

‖‖

―――

THE NEW CREATION AND CREATIVITY

But here is the good news. First, God was the one who created you to want, need, and hope for a better world. It's why your blood boils when you scroll through your newsfeed and why your heart breaks when you hear about the little boy down the street who lost his dad in a car accident. Second, God is creative and imaginative enough to make this new world for us. Remember, God is, by nature, a creator. This is something He *does* because it is part of who He *is*. This is why, as we've already seen, creativity is the first thing Scripture tells us about God and why everything that follows Genesis 2 is about His re-creation of His world.

But the redemptive work of Christ on the cross isn't the end of God's creative mission. Just as God didn't stop creating when Adam first let death into the world, God doesn't stop creating when the second Adam defeated death once and for all. Rather, God promises to make the whole world new again. He will make a new creation, inside and out.

Here's what we mean. God's work of redemptive creativity changes you, and it also changes everything in the world. Christ's re-creation leaves nothing untouched. As Abraham Kuyper famously pronounced, "There is not a square inch in the whole domain of our human existence over which Christ, who is sovereign over all, does not cry, 'Mine!'"[5] This includes your head, heart, emotions, and will—everything inside you. But it also includes everything outside of you, too: your family, the nations, rivers, mountains, art, music, dance, ants, moths, chameleons, and even everything at Disney World. Being a Christian means that God has already made you a new creation, while it also means that He is still making you a new creation, and that He is making a new creation for you. In short, God's redemptive creativity isn't aimless; it has a purpose—actually a spiritual and physical destination. He is making *you* a new creation to live eternally in *His* new creation. The God who re-created you is re-creating the world, too.

The New Creation Right Now

And God has already started His new creation. This is why Jesus talks about the kingdom of God so much in the Gospels. Christ inaugurated the kingdom, which continues to be worked out right now in the lives of His followers. Jesus used parables, stories thrown alongside truths, to illustrate His point, and to let us in on the nature of the kingdom of heaven now here on earth.

For instance, Jesus uses the parables of the mustard seed and the leaven to paint a picture of the kingdom's expansion project. Like a seed, or like leaven in flour, the kingdom that first appears small and insignificant will, with time, grow exponentially and permeate the whole world of the first Adam. Christ plants the seed of the new creation in the old. And though the old and new exist together for now (see The Parable of the Weeds, Matt. 13:24–30, 36–43), there will come a time when the kingdom of heaven will prevail against the kingdom of the serpent once and for all.

Just as the kingdom is already here but not yet in full, so God has already made you new but is also working through the Spirit to make you wholly new. The kingdom grows first and foremost in the hearts of Christ's followers.[6] Yet even though we are part of the kingdom, we are also a part of its growth—not just outwardly, but inwardly too. This is why you are saved and yet you still have to fight sin. It's why your creativity is His but you still, from time to time, want to make it yours. You are positionally His; *and*, if you're His, you're progressively becoming more like Him.

This has major implications for your life right now. It's why God calls you to grow in grace and in the knowledge of our Lord and Savior Jesus Christ (2 Peter 3:18). It is why you are supposed to present your entire self to God in response to what He has already graciously given you. You are to be a living sacrifice, holy, acceptable to God; this is your spiritual act of worship (Rom. 12:1). This means fighting against the present evil age over and over and over again so you may enjoy the promised age that is to come.

You're called to live like new creations in the old creation. Because "we have died with Christ, we believe that we will also live with him" (Rom. 6:8). This means we "must consider [ourselves] dead to sin and alive to God in Christ Jesus" (Rom. 6:11). As citizens of the kingdom, you do not let sin "reign in your mortal body," "obey its passions," or "present your members to sin as instruments for unrighteousness" (Rom. 6:12–13). Instead, you are called to present yourself to God as one who has "been brought from death to life, and your members to God as instruments for righteousness" (Rom. 6:13). Don't be conformed to this world, but be transformed by the renewal of your mind (Rom. 12:2).

The kingdom of God has broken in. The new creation is overtaking the old. That's why the gospel demands a transfer of allegiance. Those who are in Christ are no longer citizens of this world. They belong to God's kingdom (see John 17:14; Phil. 3:20; Eph. 2:19).

But this will be difficult. Because you have transferred your citizenship, you will be "sojourners and exiles" on a new exodus into the real and final Promised Land (1 Peter 2:10–11). Which puts you behind enemy lines. The world will hate you and the message of the kingdom because the world hates your King. You will face persecution and trials, not only from your enemies, but also from the fact that you still live in a broken world. Yet, because you are a citizen of heaven, your suffering isn't just for suffering's sake. No, your affliction readies you for what is to come. God is not done with you. For Christians, all purification is preparation. So take comfort that, in Christ, God is using your trials to refine you for the better creation to come. Find hope that this is just a "light momentary affliction" compared to "an eternal weight of glory" to come (2 Cor. 4:16–18). Find your joy here: that you are in God's kingdom and He is using everything in your life—*everything*—to prepare you for it.

The New Creation Yet to Come

God's redemptive creativity, however, is far more expansive than our own personal salvation and sanctification. Christ's work re-creates *all* things, including the present world marred by sin and its curses. Here is how He will do it: God promises a new heaven and new earth, one free from the curses of sin and one free for us to enjoy His presence (Isa. 65:17–26; see also Gen. 3:14–19). He will turn the world right-side up again. He will fill creation with peace once again, and struggle will be no more. In the new world of His making, "**the wolf and the lamb shall graze together; the lion shall eat straw like the ox, and dust shall be the serpent's food. They shall not hurt or destroy**" (**Isa. 65:25**). The Lord hears the groans of creation and is doing something about it.

But God isn't just making you a new creation; He is making creation new for you. This is the final hope of all that exists: that the world will be made right again—better than it was before the fall even—and God will sit enthroned at its center (Rev. 21–22). God has been working from the beginning of time to bring forth the new heavens and new earth. He who made Jerusalem is making a holy city, a New Jerusalem (Gal. 4:26; Heb. 12:22; Rev. 3:12; 21:2, 10), one that is unscathed by sin, siege, and sorrow. It is a city that knows no borders, and its gates never close. This city is our hope. God builds it for our joy and our fulfillment. He makes the new creation to be where we reside with Him, and that is the very culmination of our existence, the joy that makes our lives complete and brings us full circle back into paradise—though cosmological in scope—with our Creator and Redeemer with us in a new and better garden temple.

Like Abraham, we are looking to that "better country," "to the city . . . whose designer and builder is God" (Heb. 11:16, 10). This is the Christian's city, the one God's exiles are marching toward. **"For here we have no lasting city, but we seek the city that is to come"** (Heb. 13:14). This is the beautiful future promised that anchors everything we do at every moment of our lives. God has shown us the end of His story and is writing us closer to that end with every chapter of our lives.

WHY THE NEW CREATION MATTERS TO YOUR CREATIVITY

Creativity has always been and will always be a tool for building paradise. God made us creative to spread the beauty of Eden to the rest of the world through our creative work. The problem started when sin got in the way. When it did, we stopped building God's paradise and tried to build our own. The issue isn't that we're using our creativity to create paradise; it's that we are building the wrong one. We're using our creativity to build a dead-end road, one that ends in our own selfish gain and ingrown purposes. But God calls us to a better way. He shows us how to use our creativity to build an on-ramp onto the King's Highway, the road to the New Jerusalem.

When we do this—when we disconnect our creativity from God's new creation—it sends shockwaves through every part of our lives. You see, if there is no future hope, then our creativity either becomes shortsighted or it tries to fill the void left by God's promises on its own. When we reject God's future, we will manipulate our

> God made us creative
> to spread the beauty
> of Eden to the rest of
> the world through our
> creative work.

creativity to make another one that we try to convince ourselves will somehow overshadow His.

As a result, everything about us, including our creative work, becomes locked into this world. In an attempt to be good-natured, many of us will diligently use our creativity to try to change the world and overcome the prejudices and injustices mounting up against us. Yet notice how even this assumes God. Where do you think your impulse for justice came from, and who do you think will execute perfect and final justice when it counts? Further, for there to be lasting change, we need a world that lasts. If there is no eternity, then why does justice matter? We should just eat and drink, for tomorrow we die (see 1 Cor. 15:32). Even as we try to sweep God and His righteousness out the front door of our lives, we smuggle in assumptions about Him through the back with our attempts to make the world righteous and good through our creativity. This exposes a very important truth: the justice that so much of our creativity was meant to work toward is future-oriented and divinely determined. Justice only matters if our future matters, and our future only matters if God directs the world to His righteous ends, overcoming evil once and for all while making all things new.

Not only will we try to make a future with our creativity; we will try to make creativity our future. This happens all the time. When we are so enamored with the beauty of the world, we forget that God has offered us something better. It's like staring at a campfire that you made. Sure, it's beautiful to watch the flames dance for a time. But don't let it keep you from looking heavenward to see the night sky that God has sprinkled with stars that produce light and flame far superior to your fire. When the beauty of the world captures us for too long, we cut ourselves off from God's bigger vision for our creativity. And when this happens, we make our lives about making beautiful things for themselves. If this becomes our future, then the only things worthy of our time and our lives are our creative acts—things beautiful in the world's eyes. Without a future, we settle for what's in front of our eyes and what we produce with our hands. And when all we have are the small trinkets of our own making, we are cut off from the eternal beauty that awaits in the new heavens and new earth.

But our art cannot hold up the weight of our needs, assumptions, desires, and purpose. It was never meant to. When we try to replace God's future promises with our own creativity, we end up breaking our souls. We no longer know why we create. At best, our creativity becomes self-serving. We may talk a good game in the public square, but when we're alone, we can't help but feel empty and hollow. That's when we notice that we're not creating for God—and in many ways, not even for ourselves anymore. We're creating just to keep up appearances, to assuage the critic, to fool the masses, and to keep the money or the fame or the machine going. Our creativity has begun to re-create us, and when we're not on stage, we don't like being around the person who's always with us in the green room. And yet we continue to climb up on the rickety pedestal. We keep pushing our agenda, all while we've forgotten the reason we started doing this in the first place. In the silence, we question our art, our motives, our reasons, and our identity. But we can't stop now. Our followers wouldn't want us to, and our "creativity" won't let us.

That's the drawback of a futureless creativity. It helps us become who we want to be or what the world demands of us, but it sacrifices our God-given identity in the end. We play for the crowds or for our ego, but not for our God.

This is why the new creation is so important. God's future promises teach us that the hope of the world is not our art. It is God dwelling with humanity in the new heaven and new earth, where tears, death, mourning, crying, and pain shall be no more (Rev. 21:1–4). This perspective stops your compass of purpose, worth, and identity from spinning out of control. It gives a due north that you can point your creativity toward. Your creativity isn't your future; God is. The One who sits on the throne before a new people in the midst of a new creation is the One who holds your future and your creativity in His hands.

And this is a very good thing. First, it gives us a proper perspective. God alone is worthy. He created the world, created you, created your creativity, re-created you, re-created your creativity, and re-created the world. He gets first chair. Actually the only chair. He is the hero of *His* own story, whose powerful work writes the names of *His* people into *His* book.

And, second, it means your creativity doesn't have to hold up the world. God already does. You can rest in that now and hope in that eternally. Rest defines our experience in the new creation. Not just a quick-nap-on-Sunday type of rest but deep, anxiety-destroying, peace-inducing rest. And this new creation rest has broken into this world in many ways. There is great peace knowing that your next creative piece does not determine the trajectory of the world. It never could, and you wouldn't want it to. Which, in God's grace, gives us not just contentment but also the space we need for our creativity to flourish.

The hope of the new creation, then, should fuel your creativity with God's perspective and rest. It gives your work a proper beginning and a perfect ending. It looks back to what God started, what He re-created, and what He promises is to come. The new creation steers our creativity toward its proper destination while our creativity helps the new creation promises break into the world we now know.

Think of it this way:

The sea feels like it is yours now that you sail under the sign of the Sailmaker. The world seems more interesting, more vivid, with adventures around every corner. The old fears and temptations—the ones that led you to unhinge your sail from the mast—still float in and out of your life. But these days, their visits are less frequent and their lures less enticing. Calm and tranquility are always off your bow now, no matter the heights of the sea.

That is until the last storm.

It comes out of nowhere and is different from all the others. It feels like someone is pulling the four corners of the ocean back onto your ship. In its violence, your sail never stands a chance; the wind shreds it before you can get it off the mast. You fight to hold your position, but it's no use. The helm breaks in your hands. All that's left to do is watch the ocean swallow you whole with the eighty-foot wave that has just lifted you up, and up, and up. You close your eyes, say a prayer, and hold your breath as you await your watery death on the other side of your ascent.

But it never comes. There is no fall, no other side to the upsurge. The wave that picked you up, never puts you down. Instead, the waters level

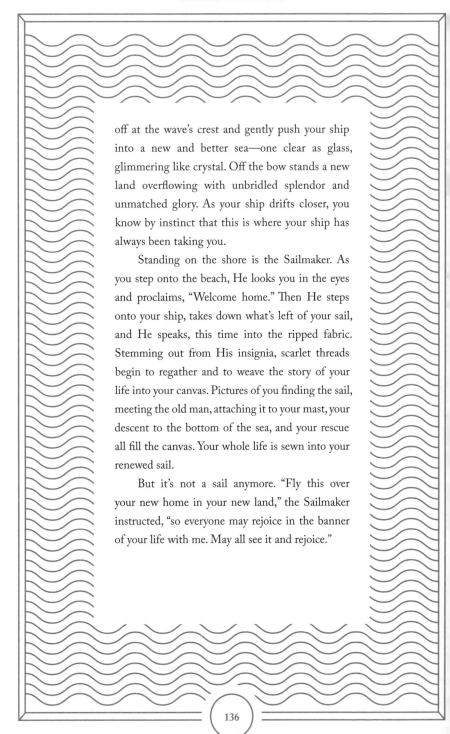

off at the wave's crest and gently push your ship into a new and better sea—one clear as glass, glimmering like crystal. Off the bow stands a new land overflowing with unbridled splendor and unmatched glory. As your ship drifts closer, you know by instinct that this is where your ship has always been taking you.

Standing on the shore is the Sailmaker. As you step onto the beach, He looks you in the eyes and proclaims, "Welcome home." Then He steps onto your ship, takes down what's left of your sail, and He speaks, this time into the ripped fabric. Stemming out from His insignia, scarlet threads begin to regather and to weave the story of your life into your canvas. Pictures of you finding the sail, meeting the old man, attaching it to your mast, your descent to the bottom of the sea, and your rescue all fill the canvas. Your whole life is sewn into your renewed sail.

But it's not a sail anymore. "Fly this over your new home in your new land," the Sailmaker instructed, "so everyone may rejoice in the banner of your life with me. May all see it and rejoice."

THE NEW CREATION AND THE PURPOSE OF YOUR CREATIVITY

Is your creativity built on future hope? If not, then it's suffering from a lack of eternal direction. Of course, it may have direction, but it's not the direction it was made to have. By the world's definition of creativity (that is, creativity without God), the Unabomber had a creative direction. So did Hitler. And before him, Emperor Nero and Ghengis Khan. We flatter ourselves when we think of creativity only in a positive light with good purposes. But we know creativity isn't just an act; it's an expression of the creative's heart. That's why you can trace this line of dark creativity all the way back to the serpent in the garden. And when we're being honest, we find traces of it in our own hearts as well. And that is why it needs the new creation. It redirects our creativity towards an eternal goal. The new creation shows us what our creativity can one day look like so we can pattern our life and work around this future vision here in our already-but-not-yet kingdom.

The New Creation and God's Glory

At the center of the new creation is God, which is why God's glory is at the center of new creation creativity. In Revelation 4, the Father is glorified for His work of creation:

> "Worthy are you, our Lord and God,
>
>> to receive glory and honor and power,
>
> for you created all things,
>
>> and by your will they existed." (v. 11)

Revelation 5 continues with a song of glory sung to the Son for His work of re-creation:

> "Worthy are you to take the scroll
>
>> and to open its seals,
>
> for you were slain, and by your blood you ransomed people
>>> for God
>
>> from every tribe and language and people and nation,
>
> and you have made them a kingdom and priests to our God,
>
>> and they shall reign on the earth." (vv. 9–10)

In the new creation, both works of creation are complete, which makes our creativity complete there as well. We are and will forever be a kingdom people, "a chosen race, a royal priesthood, a holy nation." We were made to declare and show and demonstrate the glory and beauty and "excellencies of him who called [us] out of darkness into his marvelous light" (1 Peter 2:9). Forever. The new heavens and new earth is where we are finally and fully, with no mixed motives or idolatrous tendencies, His. And in the New Jerusalem, we will be able to use our creativity, without the hindrance of sin, to worship Him in ways we want to now. And because He has done so much for us and because His worth is inexhaustible, we have fuel for our creative fires that will never run out so we can bring Him glory for all eternity in a myriad of creative ways.

But what if I told you that your creativity is only a small part of glorifying God? That your artifacts are ways to worship Him but not the sole, and perhaps not even the central, way to worship Him? You see, the new creation changes everything, even your assumptions about your creativity. We think that *we* glorify God through our creative acts. But that isn't the complete picture. Instead, God has a bigger plan for it. Your creativity has always been His. It is an instrument in His hands to glorify Himself.

This means that the point of glorifying God through your creativity isn't that you make great art for Him. Rather, it's that He uses the gifts He has given you to make you into one of His masterpieces. In the end, you are His artwork that brings Him glory. Your imagination and creativity are a part of this harmony that is your life of praise. They are just a few of the colors God uses to paint your canvas. It's just a few pieces of clay the Potter uses to make you a vessel of His glory. We can rejoice in this: God is the artist who is making us worthy to stand in the gallery of His new creation, to point to Him as our Creator and Redeemer with our life, worship, and, yes, still our creativity.

The New Creation and the World's Good

And because your creativity centers on the glory of God, it continues to be for the good of your neighbor. Like at the beginning of the world, the new creation shows you that your creativity is not primarily for evangelism. It can be, but it doesn't have to be in order to be in line with God's purposes. The key impetus of all creativity, especially in the New Jerusalem, is worship. We create to spur one another on in worship of the triune God who is no longer "out there" but "right here."

But it is different in the new creation. We don't use our creativity to enliven the heart, because our hearts will be complete in God already. We create to fuel worship, not out of duty but out of delight. It will be a pure response to God and the Lamb, an overflow of His love toward us, that will consistently spark creative expressions of our love to Him. Thus, we create to fill the world with beautiful things that reflect God's beauty. The new creation becomes a center for worship that never extinguishes and never falls short. It's like a noncompetitive one-upmanship that serves every other believer by invoking deeper praise of God and His gifts.

To many, this future experience sounds dull. Many of us want to justify our present rebellion by cutting off the joys of the future with short-term comparisons to worldly pleasures. As Lucifer in *Paradise Lost* states, "Better to reign in Hell, than to serve in Heaven."[7]

But we disagree. This view sees the world and creativity through Adam's nearsighted lenses. It doesn't see life in light of the long game, nor does it do justice to the persistent guilt that hovers over every heart that attaches itself to the world's idols. We can blame everyone and everything else for the guilt we feel, but, in the end, it doesn't go away—and for a reason. There is only One who can take it, and if we are rebels, we've made our Deliverer our enemy.

> *God can use our creativity to prop this world's doors open to the next.*

But a future-oriented creativity removes all this. Not just in the world to come but for the world right now. The kingdom means something for your creativity this very day. This is what God's future promises can do for your creativity now and what your creativity can do for others:

1. It removes anxiety surrounding your creative work.

2. It allows you to exercise your creative gifts without pretense.

3. It keeps you from the tyranny of comparisons.

4. It puts the critic in perspective as well as your audience.

5. It removes your creativity from the center of your identity.

6. It resets your motives and gives you a barometer to keep them in check.

7. It induces worship and joy before, during, and after the creative process.

8. It ties your production to eternity rather than to just the present.

9. It gives you an honest and grace-filled perspective of your work and others.

10. It makes us both responsible and reliant on the Spirit at the same time.

For those of us in God's kingdom today, then, we try to get as close to this new creation as we can. When we do, the Lord uses our glorified creativity to help bring the heavens and the earth together.

Don't misread us. We're not saying that our work will save the world. Though our creativity doesn't save sinners, our Savior does use it for His glorious purposes. Recollecting about his spiritual journey, C. S. Lewis testifies, "The sweetest thing in all my life has been the longing . . . to find the place where all the beauty came from."[8] Lewis followed this longing to the cross, where his imagination was baptized and his gifts were used to reimagine Christianity in all its beautiful orthodoxy.

As we wait for the kingdom to come, God can use our creativity to prop this world's doors open to the next. We need to let the better world in, which is why the hope of a new heaven and new earth shouldn't keep us from caring for the present world; rather, it should ground it. We can make real change in the world when we let the new world break in through our creativity. We give our gifts to God as instruments of justice and mercy.

One of the most glorious ways we can do this is by using our God-given gifts and imagination to re-enchant the world and let His transcendence shine in. This doesn't mean that we jettison truth and honesty in our art. Or that we Disney-ify all the bad things away. It means we put them in a divine order, that we combat the broken world with our creativity. We use our imaginations to make the world bigger. Our imaginations help us understand and process reality and ourselves. Our imaginations help us make sense of the world around us and give us a way to engage the transcendence. We can face our brokenness head on and we can and should do it through art, poetry, music, comedy, and the spectrum of creativity that God has given us. Creativity helps loosen the grip of the rationalistic, anti-supernatural mentality that has us by the throats so that we can breathe in the air of heaven. Our imagination is a small trapdoor God built into our humanity that allows the future to sneak into the present. But remember, the world that is to come is the world you were made for to begin with. So feel free to tell others. It's the most loving thing to do.

———

A CALL TO RECLAIMED CREATIVITY

So here at the end, we make one final appeal: let the new creation break in through your creativity. This is why you are creative and why you are called to express your creativity. Let eternity bleed through your imaginative work. Use your creativity to usher in God's better world, the one over the horizon of bare facts and constant frustration, the one your heart innately pines for.

Create like you're in the new creation, because, in a very real way, you are almost there. Your creativity is where the light of the better world breaks into the darkness of today. This is reclaimed creativity and it is why your creativity matters and how your creativity lasts. And lasts forever.

ACKNOWLEDGMENTS

While our names may appear on this book's cover, God has used many others to shape, create, and fill these pages. Both of us have been deeply influenced by the artists and staff of Humble Beast. You all live out the message of this book beautifully and have challenged us to do the same.

We both also thank God for Trinity Church of Portland. We have gone through so much together, and you have loved and encouraged us despite our weaknesses. You have been an instrument God has used to change my heart (Thomas) from a performer to a pastor.

Thanks to David Thommen, Ashton Trujillo, Bryan Winchester, Jason Petty, Jared Pulliam, Esteban Shedd, Courtland Urbano, Shai Linne, Greg Taylor, Devon Berry, Jan Verbruggen, Norm Theisen, Anthony Benedetto, and the one who helps hold Humble Beast and Thomas together, Samuel Nagel. Thank you all for your wisdom, perspective, and hard work.

To my (Thomas's) mother, who sits in the presence of our King. Thank you for your love and affirmation. Thank you for modeling authentic Christianity and how to finish well. I'll see you soon.

To my boys, Tobin Jace and Kuyper Gray. I love you and pray every day that you come to trust the One who has healed your dad in his most desperate state. I promise you that you will never have to "father figure skate."

To my wife and closest friend, Heather Terry, thank you for all the ways you love and sacrifice for the gospel and our family. Thank you for loving me as I am while simultaneously pushing to make me better. You have always been my most significant support, my biggest encouragement, and the greatest gift God has given me. Thank you.

I (Ryan) would like to thank my colleagues at Western Seminary, especially those in the Theology and Bible department who have each encouraged me along the way. I also couldn't have done this without Tyler and Sarah Velin, Chip Hardy, Kevin McFadden, and Oren Martin; each of you has reminded me of God's goodness, regardless of circumstances.

To my brother Rob, thank you for spurring me on to holiness through word and example.

To my father, Glenn, you are a great father. I hope to be half the man that you are one day, Papa G.

To my mother—to whom I've dedicated this book—even though you are with the Lord, this book remains a testimony of your consistent encouragement for me in this area. I hope you like it.

To my children, Jude, Silas, Abby Kate, and Asher. Each of you has prayed for this project and put up with me when I was daydreaming about it. You've taught me a better lesson without even knowing it: that you are, and will always be, the greatest expressions of creativity in my life. I pray this book helps you see that true happiness can be found only in God.

And to, my wife, Chase Elizabeth, you make me want to know Jesus better and remind me of the brilliant world beyond my anxieties. Thank you for reading every word of this book, highlighting the weaknesses, rejoicing in the strengths, and reminding me that none of this matters if it's not for God's glory. Thank you, even more, for doing this for my life too.

Finally, this book wouldn't exist if it weren't for the help and guidance of Drew Dyck and the rest of the team at Moody Publishers. Thank you, Drew, for believing in this project and in us. Moody, thank you for making this project your own.

NOTES

Creativity Begins with God

1. "Christian Recording Artist Still On Track To Renounce Faith By 2018," *Babylon Bee*, March 10, 2017, http://babylonbee.com/news/christian-recording-artist-still-track-renounce-faith-2018/.

2. Amy M. Azzam, "Why Creativity Now? A Conversation with Sir Ken Robinson," *Educational Leadership* 67, no. 1 (2009): 22.

01
The Creator of Creativity— What God Has to Do with Your Creativity

1. Dr. Robin Rosenberg, a clinical psychologist who wrote a book on superhero origins, defines them this way: "an origin story explains who someone is, what's made the person that way, what the person cares about and why." See Rosenberg, *Superhero Origins: What Makes Superheroes Tick and Why We Care* (Scotts Valley, CA: CreateSpace, 2013), 1.

2. Natalie Haynes connects ancient mythology with Marvel's origin

stories this way: "Every super-hero has his origin story, and a surprisingly large number of modern ones owe those origins to myths of gods and heroes who existed millennia before their cultural descendants. Even Ant-Man isn't a completely re-cent phenomenon: Zeus turned himself into an ant, as part of his scheme to have sex with every pretty girl in the ancient world while disguised as an array of different creatures. Leda was ravished by him in swan form; poor Eurymedusa was accosted by him as an ant. Achilles' war-riors, the Myrmidons, legendarily owe their name to this union (the Greek word for an ant is *myrmex*): they too are Ant-men." See Natalie Haynes, "Before Marvel and DC: Superheroes of the ancient world," *BBC*, August 19, 2015, http://www.bbc.com/culture/story/20150819-before-marvel-and-dc-superheroes-of-the-ancient-world.

3. We are even at the point that Marvel has already begun rebooting the origin stories of the origin stories they told only a few years ago. One such franchise that can't seem to stop is *Spider-Man*. Since 2002, Marvel has given us seven Spider Man movies with more on the way, two of which interpret Peter Parker's genesis as the reluctant teenage wall crawler (2002, 2012), while the newest installment appears poised for a flashback. See Eliana Dockterman, "Here's Why Hollywood Will Never Stop Making Spider-Man Movies," *Time*, June 2017, http://time.com/4784729/spiderman-homecoming-sony-marvel-reboot/.

4. But it isn't just Marvel. Star Wars recently moved its franchise forward by going back to a galaxy far, far away to fill in the plot lines in its original trilogy with movies like *Rogue One*. And with over twenty movies already in weekly circulation on basic cable, James Bond wasn't immune to the backstory treatment in 2006's *Casino Royale*. Even the creative geniuses at Pixar sought to capitalize on this trend in 2013 by taking their audience back to school to *Monsters University* to tell the story of Mike and Sulley's unlikely friendship that formed the backbone of the 2001 original *Monsters, Inc.*

5. We love that they give us new (and nostalgic) worlds. Why else do people cheer when they see the opening crawl of Star Wars? They reveal motives and provide insights that help us grow closer to our ink and celluloid cast

friends (we strike out with Frodo because we've already been on adventures with his uncle Bilbo and the one ring in *The Hobbit*). Perhaps, most importantly, origin stories connect us to what is to be and help reveal what we were even looking for in the first place (Harry Potter is the boy who lived in the first book, so he can be the boy who dies in the last book).

6. Joseph Campbell with Bill Moyers, *The Power of Myth* (New York: Doubleday, 1988), 53.

7. Søren Kierkegaard, *Papers and Journals*, trans. Alastair Hannay (New York: Penguin, 1996), 63.

8. We recognize the risk. Some will undoubtedly criticize us of collapsing all of who God is into His creativity, whereas others are sure to offer praise for the exact same reason. To be clear from the outset, we spotlight this attribute, not over and against others, but because it is the linchpin of reclaimed creativity. We do so because theologians often miss it, and we do so because creatives often want it expunged from the conversation as a whole. Omission and abolition are both creative dead ends. Rooting our lives in the deep soil of God's character benefits both our theology and our creativity. In

other words, the reward is greater than the risk. Highlighting God's creativity ultimately frees us to do what God made us to do, while His creativity shows us how to sing our theology.

9. We need to ensure we don't equate God with an image. There are limitations, and these are tied to our humanity and sin, not to God Himself. Metaphors are a part of God's communicative and revelatory grace. They "do not circumscribe our understanding of God, but rather are an open door to understanding that our finite conceptions of God are only a crack in the door through which we peer into the vastness of God's nature" (Gene Fant, *God as Author: A Biblical Approach to Narrative* [Nashville: B&H Academic, 2010], 42). Metaphors are the mirror in which we see God dimly. And yet we still can see God through the imagery God uses to reveal Himself.

10. John Calvin, *Commentary on the Psalms* in *Calvin's Commentaries*, vol. 4 (Grand Rapids: Baker, 1999), 309.

11. Ibid.

12. Donald Guthrie, *The Letter to the Hebrews: An Introduction and Commentary*, volume 15

(Downers Grove, IL: InterVarsity Press, 1983), 234.

13. God is the first art critic and ultimately the only one who can properly evaluate and judge the value of his work, and ours.

14. Jonathan Edwards (sorry, Propaganda: the Puritans still have a few good things to say) puts it this way: "For as God is infinitely the greatest Being, so he is allowed to be infinitely the most beautiful and excellent: and all beauty to be found throughout the whole creation is but the reflection of the diffused beams of that Being who has an infinite fulness of brightness and glory. God . . . the foundation and fountain of all being and all beauty" (Jonathan Edwards, *A Dissertation on the Nature of True Virtue* in *The Works of Jonathan Edwards*, vol. 1 (Peabody, MA: Hendrickson, 1998), 125.

15. The Hebrew word for "potter" shares the same lexical roots as the Hebrew verb for "formed" in Genesis 2:7. This passage highlights God's artistry in creating man, and we would argue that it is the first image of God as Potter that plays out over the rest of Scripture (for example, Isa. 64:8).

16. We will return to this idea in the chapters to come. For now, though, it is important to see not only that God is the artist who creates all things, but also that He uses the image of the Artist to unveil His character and work from the first creation to the new creation.

17. Edmund Clowney, *The Message of 1 Peter: The Way of the Cross* (Downers Grove, IL: InterVarsity Press, 1988), 76.

18. For further reading, see D. A. Carson, *The Gospel according to John* (Leicester, England: Inter-Varsity Press; Grand Rapids: Wm. B. Eerdmans, 1991), 116.

19. Augustine, *Concerning the Nature of Good, Against the Manicheans,* in *Nicene and Post Nicene-Fathers*, First Series, vol. 4, ed. Philip Schaff (Peabody, MA: Hendrickson, 1996), 351.

02

Created to Create—What Your Humanity Has to Do with Your Creativity

1. *Ratatouille* (2007).

2. "Brad Bird Interview – Ratatouille," YouTube, February 19, 2016, https://www.youtube.com/watch?v=imyixSTo0tQ.

3. "Ratatouille Brad Bird Interview!," YouTube, June 28, 2007, https://www.youtube.com/watch?v=OY5zA6yS_9k.

4. Ed Catmull, *Creativity, Inc: Overcoming the Unseen Forces That Stand in the Way of True Inspiration* (New York: Random House, 2014), 144.

5. Ibid., 131 (emphasis added).

6. Austin Kleon, *Steal Like an Artist*, (New York: Workman Publishing, 2012), 5, charmingly observes, "Every artist gets asked the question, 'Where do you get your ideas?' The honest artist answers, 'I steal them.'"

7. In fact, Pixar outright attacks manufactured humanity in their 2008 film *WALL-E*, where, yet again, they set out to shock us back into personhood with a charming, trash-compacting robot who, like Remy in *Ratatouille*, shows a technologically gluttonous community what the true, good, and beautiful life really is like.

8. Anthony A. Hoekema, *Created in God's Image* (Grand Rapids: Eerdmans, 1986), 4. To most creatives, this sounds like entrapment, but in actuality, this structure brings freedom by allowing us to create based on our creativity's original design.

9. John Calvin, *Institutes of the Christian Religion*, ed. John T. McNeill, trans. Ford Lewis Battles (Louisville: WJK Press, 2006), 1.1.2.

10. Dorothy Sayers, "The Image of God," in *The Mind of the Maker* (San Francisco: HarperOne, 1987), 22.

11. This also means our creativity is part of God's mission. Progression is at the center of God's creation from the beginning, as His mandate to Adam and Eve makes clear. Genealogical growth (be fruitful and multiply) demands geographical advancement (fill the earth and subdue it). God's garden sanctuary—the focus of His creative work—may have begun as a small plot of land in the Middle East, but it was always meant to cover the face of all the earth. The singular mechanism of this is the image of God in man. This is why God plants Adam and Eve in Eden and yet commands them to exercise dominion over all the earth. This is why Adam and Eve are to fill the earth with more image bearers. A worldwide expansion project demands all of

our creativity and requires a lot more image bearers who can use their God-given creativity for God's cosmological drama.

12. J. R. R. Tolkien, "On Fairy-Stories," in *Tree and Leaf*, in *The Tolkien Reader* (New York: Ballantine Books, 2001), 75.

13. Francis A. Schaeffer, *Art and the Bible* (Downers Grove, IL: InterVarsity Press, 2006), 43.

14. Kory Grow, "Robin Thicke, Pharrell Lose Multi-Million Dollar 'Blurred Lines' Lawsuit," *Rolling Stone*, March 10, 2015, https://www.rollingstone.com/music/music-news/robin-thicke-pharrell-lose-multi-million-dollar-blurred-lines-lawsuit-35975/.

15. At the dedication of the temple, Solomon again recognizes his reliance on God in his creative accomplishment: "But who am I, and what is my people, that we should be able thus to offer willingly? For all things come from you, and of your own have we given you" (1 Chron. 29:14).

16. Augustine, *Confessions*, trans. Henry Chadwick (New York: Oxford University Press, 2009), 3.

17. Unlimited freedom and unlimited creativity are both misnomers, and both misleading. Regarding creativity, you need discipline, a system, and a proper imagination in order to accomplish your creative goals. Without them, there is no way, place, or mechanism for your creativity to thrive and move the world forward.

18. We imagine that this chapter has made many of you bristle a little—or maybe a lot. As a creative, you're supposed to break barriers, not live behind them. You're in the business of overturning the status quo, not acquiescing to it. The problem with this is that any creativity requires discipline and understanding the framework before you can change it. Creativity, then, that is unaccountable to anything is irresponsible, regardless of your spiritual convictions.

19. The Greek term for image is *eikōn*, which forms the origin for our English word icon. Further, the Hebrew cognate (*ṣĕ·lĕm*) is derived from the root that means "to carve out" or "to cut," and when used outside the context of humanity, it applies to idols (see Num. 33:52; 2 Kings 11:18; 2 Chron. 23:17; Ezek. 7:20; 16:17; 23:14).

20. And, no, our madness—like Denathor's—hasn't set in at this point yet, but it's coming in the next chapter.

21. Tim Keller, "Why We Need Artists," in *It Was Good: Making Art to the Glory of God*, ed. Ned Bustard (Baltimore: Square Halo Books, 2006), 120.

22. Ibid. Or as Pablo Casals puts it into a sentence: "Music is the divine way to tell beautiful, poetic things to the heart."

23. Anne Lamott, *Help, Thanks, Wow: The Three Essential Prayers* (New York: Riverhead Books, 2012), 83.

24. Keller, "Why We Need Artists," 120.

25. There are, of course, youthful rejoinders, like the "what if we leave our good construction on the floor" argument, to which we break out the "then it is not good enough to be off the floor" retort.

26. This land is your land, to preserve and protect through creativity (Gen. 1:28; 2:15; 9:1–3; Ps. 8:6–8; 115:16; Heb. 2:8; James 3:7).

27. We will address the concept of creativity and culture at length in the third volume of this series.

03
The Corruption of Creativity— What Sin Has to Do with Your Creativity

1. Examples of this include *The Wizard of Oz*; *Gone with the Wind*; *The Hobbit*; *A Christmas Story*; *James Bond* (take your pick); and Thomas's personal favorites, *Spaceballs* and *Thelma & Louise*.

2. Many attribute the formal concept of "Art for Art's Sake" to nineteenth-century philosopher Victor Cousin, who coined his own French phrase, *l'art pour l'art*, with the same meaning. Influenced by Romanticism, Cousin and others sought to unhinge art from the "tyranny of rationalism" and, in doing so, paved the way for art's autonomy and current (seemingly) anarchistic expressions. In America, the nineteenth-century poet Edgar Allan Poe was making similar arguments for poetry. In his essay "The Poetic Principle," Poe argues, "We have taken it into our heads that to write a poem simply for the poem's sake, and to acknowledge such to have been our design, would be to confess ourselves radically wanting in the true poetic dignity and force: — but the simple fact is that, would we but permit ourselves to look into our own souls, we should

immediately there discover that under the sun there neither exists nor can exist any work more thoroughly dignified, more supremely noble, than this very poem, this poem per se, this poem which is a poem and nothing more, this poem written solely for the poem's sake." Edgar Allan Poe, "The Poetic Principle" in *The Works of the Late Edgar Allan Poe*, vol. 2, ed. N. P. Willis and J. R. Lowell (New York: Redfield, 1856), xi.

3.   Hans R. Rookmaaker, *Art Needs No Justification* (Vancouver, BC: Regent College Publishing, 2010), 11.

4.   Ibid., 13.

5.   Tim Keller, "Preaching Hell in a Tolerant Age," in *Is Hell for Real or Is Everyone Going to Heaven?*, eds. Chris Morgan and Robert Peterson (Grand Rapids: Zondervan, 2011), 77.

6.   Philip Graham Ryken, *Art for God's Sake: A Call to Recover the Arts* (Phillipsburg, PA: P&R, 2006), 12.

7.   C. S. Lewis, *The Great Divorce* in The Complete C. S. Lewis Signature Classics (San Francisco: HarperOne, 2002), 343.

8.   Flannery O'Connor, *Mystery and Manners*, eds. Sally and Robert Fitzgerald (New York: Noonday Press, 1969), 173–174.

9.   R. C. Sproul, *Lifeviews: Make a Christian Impact on Culture and Society* (Grand Rapids: Revell, 1995), 164.

10. Brett McCracken, *Hipster Christianity: When Church and Cool Collide* (Grand Rapids: Baker, 2010), 167.

11. C. S. Lewis, "The Weight of Glory," in *The Weight of Glory* (San Francisco: HarperOne, 2001), 32.

12. Neil Gaiman, *Make Good Art* (New York: William Morrow. 2013), 45.

04

Creativity Re-Created—What Jesus Has to Do with Your Creativity

1.   Mark Zuckerberg, "Building Global Community," Facebook, February 16, 2017, https://www .facebook.com/notes/mark-zuckerberg/building-global-community/10154544292806634/.

2.   Ibid.

3.   Mark Zuckerberg, "Bringing the World Closer Together,"

Facebook, June 22, 2017, https://www.facebook.com/ notes/mark-zuckerberg/ bringing-the-world-closer-together/10154944663901634/.

4. Ibid.

5. Zuckerberg, "Building Global Community."

6. As Zuckerberg himself explains, "I always believed people are basically good. As I've traveled around, I've met all kinds of people from regular folks to heads of state, and I've found they almost all genuinely care about helping people" ("Bringing the World Closer Together").

7. This is the very reason why Facebook is employing artificial intelligence, to uproot the sins of fake news and terrorist cells on their platform, all the while turning a blind eye to these communities that lie outside the utopian communities Zuckerberg will support. This is the curse of a relativistic society, however. Without any grounds for what is good and what is bad, all communities end up being fair game—at least in theory.

8. See chapter 2 for this corrective. In short, we have to recognize that we do great and creative things because we bear the image of our creative God, but simultaneously we see how our sin has broken that image and twisted these great and creative things into our self-made despotic gods.

9. Christ is also reenacting Israel's drama in the wilderness.

10. In John 1:14, the gospel writer uses a verb (*skēnoō*) that, when more literally translated, means that Jesus set up the tabernacle in his flesh. This word choice signals that Jesus' entering into the world fulfilled the vision and purpose of the tabernacle— namely, that God was present with and for His people.

11. Creative imagery is everywhere in the New Testament. It doesn't just detail Christ's work in the Gospels; it also teaches Christians about how they know where they're supposed to belong. It's why the church is the new temple, the body of Christ, God's household, and Jesus' bride. It's why Christ Himself is the church's chief architect (Matt. 16:18) and cornerstone (Eph. 2:20).

12. See Isaac Watts, "When I Survey the Wondrous Cross," 1707, Timeless Truths, https://

library.timelesstruths.org/music/
When_I_Survey_the_Wondrous_
Cross/.

13. For more interaction on
the bronze serpent, art, and
Christianity, see the helpful
reflections in this volume, Gene
Edward Veith, Jr., *State of the
Arts: From Bezalel to Mapplethorpe*
(Wheaton, IL: Crossway, 1991),
204–207, 222–24.

14. And reign over us it does. Slowly
but surely it creeps its way onto
the throne of our lives in the
quiet moments when all we can
see and hear is the hypocrisy and
ugliness of other Christians, how
limiting theology is, and how
the world seems so much more
entranced with beauty than God's
simpleminded, clichéd followers.

15. Leo Tolstoy, *What is Art?*, trans.
Aylmer Maude (New York:
Thomas Y. Crowell, 1899), 183.

16. Sherwood Anderson, *Letters of
Sherwood Anderson*, ed. Howard
Mumford Jones (New York:
Little, Brown, and Company,
1953), 166.

17. Frida Kahlo, *The Letters of Frida
Kahlo: Cartas Apasionadas*, ed.
Martha Zamora (San Francisco:
Chronicle Books, 1995), 157.

18. Jeremy Adam Smith and
Jason Marsh, "Why We Make
Art," *Greater Good Magazine*,
December 1, 2008, https://
greatergood.berkeley.edu/article/
item/why_we_make_art.

19. Fyodor Dostoevsky, *The Idiot*
(Hertfordshire: Wordsworth
Editions, 1998), 492.

20. To be sure, the modern
church has, in many ways,
underemphasized and hurt the
creative side of the Christian.
There is almost a "please leave
your artistic bent at the door"
sign in many churches' foyers.
In large part, this is due to the
didactic mode of the church
predominant in the West, a
mantra of "if you get their minds
into heaven then you get all of
them into heaven." But as the
culture shifts its center from the
mind to the emotions, the church
is missing its target audience
and, in many ways, speaking a
different language. Recognizing
and appreciating (notice we are
not saying idolizing) the creative
worldview as one in the pews
would help reach the world
for God's glory and, not only
that, deepen our concepts of
theology proper and theological
anthropology so that our pastoral
care actually matters. It is able to
speak both the language of the

heart and the mind as these are not separated in God as they are oftentimes in the culture.

21. This doesn't mean that Christians will be the best artists, but it does mean that Christians will know the One behind their love of art and have art in its proper perspective.

22. G. K. Chesterton, "A Defense of China Shepherdesses," in *The Defendant* (London: J.M. Dent & Sons, 1918), 84.

23. This is because of the expansive reach of Christ's person and work. The gospel is about God's provision of eternal life, but it is also about His provision for your life right now. The gospel encompasses all of you—it transforms everything, including your creativity and the dreams you have for your creativity. It turns your creativity inside out. It breaks its idolatry and forces its outward glance.

05

The Crescendo of Creativity— What the New Creation Has to Do With Your Creativity

1. Walt Disney quoted in Priscilla Hobbs, *Walt's Utopia: Disneyland and American Mythmaking*

(Jefferson, NC: McFarland & Company, 2015), 127.

2. Eve Zibart, *Inside Disney: The Incredible Story of Walt Disney World and the Man Behind the Mouse* (Hoboken, NJ: Wiley, 2002), 33.

3. David Greusel, "Disney World and Designing God's Kingdom," Think Christian, September 1, 2016, https://thinkchristian .reframemedia.com/disney- world-and-designing-gods- kingdom.

4. Mike P., "Is This What Heaven Is Like?" Oh My Disney, https://ohmy.disney.com/ insider/2014/09/15/is-this-what- heaven-is-like/.

5. Abraham Kuyper, "Inaugural Address at the Dedication of the Free University," in *Abraham Kuyper: A Centennial Reader*, ed. James D. Bratt (Grand Rapids: Eerdmans, 1998), 488.

6. This is what the parable of the sower illustrates so ingeniously. The seed of the kingdom sown on the path, the rocky ground, and among the thorns can't survive; only the seed that falls on the good soil will spring up and last. So too is it with the good news of the kingdom. It

will not last in hard hearts of
the scribes and Pharisees, or
in the hearts of those who run
from God in persecution or in
those who let the cares of the
world strangle it. The kingdom
of heaven survives only in the
hearts that know God's Word,
understand it, and produce fruit
from it.

7. John Milton, *Paradise Lost*, ed.
    John Leonard (New York, NY:
    Penguin Group, 2000), 296.

8. C. S. Lewis, *Till We Have Faces:
    A Myth Retold* (San Francisco:
    HarperOne, 2017), 86.

THE RECLAIMING CREATIVITY SERIES

As a book series, *Reclaiming Creativity* exists to help restore creativity to God's original vision. We want to hit the reset button on the faith-creativity problem and help creativity be what God intended it to be: a composite of beauty, worship, and service.

To do this, the series explores how *Reclaiming Creativity* transforms a principal sphere of the Christian life—namely, creativity's relationship with God, the church, and the culture.

In exploring creativity's relationship with God, we respond to two questions. First, what does God have to do with your creativity? And second, what does your creativity have to do with God? The answers, we have found, are tied to the drama of redemption. God, our Creator of creativity, created us in His *image* to be creative. Yet we've turned our creativity into an *idol*, forsaking our Creator for the creative gift. And so begins a theology of creativity that we apply to your creative lives.

This series also seeks to bridge the divide between the church and the creative. For the skeptical pastor and parishioner, we will work to show how the creative mind equips the church and energizes the Christian faith. For the skeptical creative struggling with the church, we want to help clarify that their assumed ecclesiological problems can actually fuel a sanctified imagination and a cross-wrought humility for the good of others and even our creative acts.

Finally, this series seeks to help creatives think through what it means to paint divine light onto the world's dark canvas. We seek to process what sanctified imagination offers a post-Christian culture. We want to help creatives think about the big questions Christians face regarding their creativity. For example, what are Christians supposed to do with their creativity? Assimilation? Provocation? Evangelism? Finally, we want to help combat the culture's war on Christianity (and vice versa) with a better creativity, one that offers the world what is truly true, truly good, and truly beautiful.